50 Seeds

GERMAINE MOODY

50 Seeds of Greatness by Germaine Moody.

ISBN-13: 968-0615867472
ISBN-10: 0615867472

Table Of Greatness

Seed 31: CHANGE YOUR ATMOSPHERE
pg 407

Seed 32: THE JOURNEY   421

Seed 40: A CLEAR VIEW FROM THE MOUNTAIN pg 519

Seed 41: THE ABUNDANCE MIND   533

Seed 42: IF YOU CAN HELP SOMEONE, HELP THEM pg 547

Thank You. Gracias. Dankie. Hvala. Dekuji. Grazie. Paldies.
Obrigado. Koszonom. Terima Casi. Dziekuje.

I would like to thank everyone who had anything to do with

the development and completion of this book. Together we traveled and now we have arrived at new realm of possibilities. I dedicate *50 Seeds of Greatness* to my mother Geraldine Brown and all the moms around the world. Let it be known that what you do as a caring, nurturing and supportive mother, throughout the life of your children, is Greatness all by itself. We thank you.

To my global team that works so diligently, with excellence and precision, vision and clarity, creativity and innovation, sacrifice and dedication, to help me do what I do, all of you are amazing, immovable giants, God's generals, and true legends in my eyes.

To the visionaries, humanitarians, philanthropists, missionaries, volunteers, medical teams, all those who use their lives to better the lives of others in times of crises and on a daily basis, you are Greatness.

To the global contributors that participated in this force of publishing, thank you for helping me produce hope in the hearts of the people, sending life-changing power to kick down the front doors and enter homes around the world. May wisdom, knowledge, understanding, peace, awareness, abundance, and immeasurable faith be with you all from this day forward.

-Germaine Moody

Introduction

10:09am - Time to be Great.

You've opened the door for not only hope, opportunity and expansion within your life but you've also added more coals to the fire for this amazing movement of motivation, inspiration, empowerment and brotherhood across planet Earth. *50 Seeds of Greatness* has been a remarkable and eye-opening journey for me, one of great excitement, supernatural energy, daily awe, and unruly emotions. I've shed many tears during the development of this project, witnessing hundreds of touching submissions come in from around the world, also emails, phone calls, text messages, Skype calls, instant messages and more from supporters telling me how much this has given them hope and reason to continue on their journey of life. All of this has made me think, wonder, meditate, and seek an answer as to why I was chosen to lead such an significant project. As of today I can finally answer that question, this is what I was born to do. Something within my soul and spirit literally forced me to do it. I've sacrificed sleep, my personal life, the everyday outside world, even food at times, just to stay on track to meet a heart-wrenching and internally convicting deadline to produce what you are about to read.

Throughout *50 Seeds of Greatness*, you'll see over three hundred contributions by business professionals from more than 100 countries worldwide. With those will appear a time of day (ex. 4:43pm), representing the exact moment we received their message via email in the USA. Morning, noon, evening/night and late night/early morning hours all came in, validating that Greatness is not on a schedule, it is forever present in us, every hour of the day, awaiting release. You'll also come across short one-page sections entitled "Be Bold", "Be Wise", and "Be Great". These include a few of the profound points or words that stood out to me in the book.

I must confess, the processes and circumstances that my life had to endure before I could honestly release this book were very frustrating, painful and heartbreaking, a humbling like no other, yet I gained new insight, vision and awareness I never knew existed. From these experiences I believe I've tapped into an unlimited power that can light the entire world. Now I'd like to share that power with you, your family, your friends, and your future, in this easy to read book, with the help of my friends around the world joining me.

No matter what happens in your life, desire to be greater. Whatever situations you encounter, especially those that bring distress, disappointment or aggravation, seek to learn from them and become greater every time. I believe that's our common bond, the desire to be better and to grow, as a people, as humanity. We alone hold the true treasures in this world. The greatest treasure is what we can do together, as a team, as a force, upon the land, across the seas, in one accord. Let us be mindful of this moment and aware of what has been accomplished, not only in this book but also on this planet, by and in the hearts of many who helped make this into a tangible reality. If we share it, this message can touch millions, even billions, from generation to generation. We have created history and now you are a part of it. We have lived Greatness and now it's your time to be Great.

August 15, 2013

50 Seeds of Greatness

GERMAINE MOODY

BE Become Endless

Seed 1
TIMING

TIMING

There is beauty in every second. It all depends on how you view your daily moments of self-realization. Everything happens when it is allowed by the author of time, Almighty God. There is no rush, there are no setbacks and no delays. Take a deep breath. Now release your mental schedule for your life. It is important to plan but it is even more important to flow during the process. Some things in life will only be manifested during the flow and season of its respected timing, and not during our set or scheduled timing. Flow in the beauty of every second. Then with timing, everything else in your life will develop as it should, minute by minute.

- **Seed Description:** The awareness of Timing

- **Soil:** Plant this into your daily life and use it to make quality time-sensitive decisions.

- **Water:** Water it with observation, patience and alertness, research, plus learning from your mistakes and the mistakes of others.

- **Oxygen:** Practice your awareness of timing in all things. It could be as simple as preparing for a storm when you notice dark clouds in the sky or rehearsing your answers to questions before an interview. The more you practice, the more you will begin to become a master in this realm, and it will eventually overflow into the biggest areas of your life; family, career, purpose and mission.

- **Temperature:** When you know the season is right and the moment is before you, by all means go in for the attack and strike while it's hot.

- **Light/Darkness:** We must be willing to accept a multiplicity of circumstances and situations, highs and lows, good and bad, to grow the seed of timing.

- **Dormancy:** When it's hard to recognize the right timing, you wait, patiently. Refuel your inner man, continue to grow internally and remain curious.

- **Germination:** Support its growth by taking calculated, time-sensitive risks and trusting your spiritual instinct.

New Zealand

"Just as beauty is in the eye of the beholder, Greatness is attributed to us by those we have influenced; only because we were at first influenced by someone Great ourselves. Greatness therefore stands on the shoulders of the wisdom of all those who have walked this path before us. Greatness creates a platform, a firm foundation from which it reaches out a helping hand to lift up anyone who seeks to be inspired to go beyond their limitation, perceived or otherwise and onto some astonishing new height for the benefit of all human kind. Ultimately the more seeds of Greatness we have planted that took root and flourished, is more the true measure and the testimony to how great we may have been."

-Glyn MacLean

National Channel Manager – Attache Business Improvement Advisory at Attache Software

San Francisco, California

United States of America

"Everyone has the seeds of greatness, and the seeds of their own downfall. Cultivation of greatness requires a rigorous preference for your own senses and feelings over mental chatter and conditioned fear. Every moment contains the choice of which seed to water. Repeatedly choosing your own senses and feelings trains your mind to stay open, curious, sensitive and deeply connected with the seeds of greatness in all beings."

-Miko Matsumura

SVP Platform Marketing and Developer Relations

Scarborough, Ontario
Canada

"Greatness is the ability to rise above and beyond all obstacles encountered on your journey to success. It means coming out of your shell and comfort zone to achieve something extraordinary. Greatness is looking at fear in the face and saying I will conquer."

-Jane Iwenofu

Author

BE BOLD.

You must push through the gate to discover more than what the lazy mind wants to work to receive. You must knock down the boundaries around mediocre thinking, then run out and capture unlimited thinking, so that your life can resemble what is within you.

Atlanta, Georgia

United States of America

"Greatness is not what you do, but who you are, your nature, the very essence of your being. It originates from a declaration of the One who's greater and it is determined by the acceptance of that declaration."

-George Moody

CEO MOODY Marketing Firm

Tonbridge, Kent England
United Kingdom

"Greatness is to stand firm in my beliefs and be respected for my honesty when dishonesty would be more profitable."

-Susi Ibelati

Copywriter

Chicago, Illinois
United States of America

"Greatness is... waking up everyday with the courage to persistently follow your heart and your dreams. It is the desire to learn and improve yourself on a daily basis, inspiring those around you. It is the ability to be successful and possess inner confidence, while being humble towards others and appreciating a helping hand when needed. It is a natural instinct to want to help other people, when knowing they cannot give anything in return. Greatness is the power to never blame anyone for the events in your life, taking responsibility for your actions and having the willpower to make changes in your life."

-Elena Chernyakova

Actress

Stockholm

Sweden

"Greatness is when things you accomplish, both professionally and personally, becomes of a substantial meaning to someone else."

-Peter Hjort

Country Manager Pulse Communications

Seed 2
PREPARATION

PREPARATION

Life doesn't slow down just because we're tired or restless, it will move on just fine whether we participate or not. Those that prepare for what life could bring seem to live more peaceful lives. There is always something you can do to prepare for the next day. Why would you want to live unprepared anyway? Prepare for what you want. Prepare for what you don't want. It's like carrying around an internal business plan. Read it over and over, make adjustments when necessary, and follow it. This way you can quickly stop and observe at the red lights, then take off and soar at the green ones.

- **Seed Description:** Preparation

- **Soil:** Plant this into everyday life. When you have free time from your normal routine, make time to prepare for something else. It may be a new career, hobby, pursuit or anything you desire to accomplish in your lifetime.

- **Water:** Water it by making a schedule so that you actually get it done. We all talk about doing this and that, then never do it. You have to be determined, as in a life or death situation, to block out time for preparation. You will never see your goal come to pass if you don't.

- **Oxygen:** Having a driven mindset keeps the wind of preparation blowing. Wake up knowing that each day you prepare, your chances of getting closer and closer to what it is you desire to achieve are far greater than not preparing at all.

- **Temperature:** There will be long seasons of preparation in your life where it seems the goal at hand will never be accomplished. There are also seasons where all your preparation will pay off. You must be mindful of the sacrifice involved before preparation on any matter. Sometimes you'll know how long it will take, other times you will just have to prepare and stay prepared until it happens.

- **Light/Darkness:** Preparation can produce great loneliness and even depression if not careful, so as with pursuing anything of great value, it's smart to surround yourself with others who are also preparing for something, this activates encouragement and support.

- **Dormancy:** In times where you feel like you aren't getting anywhere, continue anyway. Preparation is not the goal, it part of the process to reach the goal, so don't expect to be excited every single day, though I hope you will be. Days when you feel least motivated are the testings of greatness. Everyone would continue if they saw the finish line in front of them. When that line is nowhere in sight for days, hours, months or even years, only those who have sacrificed tremendously and prepared diligently will remain to complete the race.

- **Germination:** Support its growth by noticing the benefits of preparation in all things. Even by studying the lives, accomplishments and creations of others, you will be empowered by the advantages of preparation.

New York, New York
United States of America

"Greatness is an honor bestowed on someone who has made the world a better place by unselfishly helping and benefiting his or her fellow man and is a title not given to oneself but to others. True greatness is anonymous."

-David L. Morehead

Executive Director at Calling From The Dream

Barbados

"Greatness is the ultimate destination reached through life's journey. It is not measured by individual wealth or success but by the lessons learnt on our path to self-appreciation."

-Natasha 'Nyah' Adams

Start-up Business Consultant

Olmsted, Ohio

United States of America

"By its very definition, greatness refers to a natural largess that encompasses a variety of meanings (size, quality, emotion, and influence.) But understanding its true ramifications as it applies to everyday life requires a different lexicon. Residing within each of us is a well of untapped strength bursting with potential and patiently waiting to aid us in our journey. The path is different for each person— many are content in their aspirations for fame and fortune as a measure for greatness. But to me, true greatness does not require grandiose plans–merely the ability to touch the heart of another."

-Mary Frances Fisher

Author | Nurse Consultant North

Singapore

"Greatness gives the power to influence, inspire and empower others to take action or a chain of actions towards greatness. This impact can occur long after the original source of greatness has past current times."

-James Lee

Entrepreneur | Visionary

BE WISE.

Make it mandatory, as much as possible, to surround yourself with people and things that release positive words around you and into your life. This is the audible key of greatness. Without it, you will be locked out of inner wealth while remaining trapped into the world's fascination with poverty, drama and dismay.

Miami, Florida
United States of America

"Greatness means having the three P's in life: Patience to wait for great moments of life both personal & professional. Practice, because to achieve any feat of greatness one must practice until it hurts. Lastly we have peace, for the simple fact that without peace of mind you will lack patience & without patience you will never practice."

-Jorge A. Perez

Recording Artist "DC Cruz"

Ukraine

"Living in a modern society, we often forget the true values of life. We forget the simple joys and simple concepts. For me, the greatness, in the first place, is the ability to understand, to forgive, to help, and believe not only in himself, but in the other person. And only by understanding the real truth of relations, and rethinking of the true values, can greatness be experienced."

-Alexandr Jdanov

Owner Alex & Co.

Las Vegas, Nevada

United States of America

"Greatness is an action, the recurring ability to look at not just yourself but at the world for all of its potential, from the bleak negatives to the grays of understanding to the bountiful positives and choosing time and time again to nurture, aggressively, the positive and convert, aggressively, the negative into benefits."

-Daria Amai Shelton

Co-Founder of USR Media LV

Seed 3

RESPECT

RESPECT

It seems as though our world has lost touch with the

brotherhood of mankind. Thankfully, there are still some who continue to carry the torch for decency and appreciation for all human beings. In life, it is important to acknowledge that we were all placed here together, to learn, to love and to live. Accepting this truth grants you peace and the upper hand when dealing with many of today's problems that all too often produce frustration for most. By respecting the breath of life that is shared, you become one with everything. This is turn allows what you desire and need to be drawn to you. Whatever you release, it shall be returned to you even more. Hold your torch high. You have the power to light the darkest places of the human soul and lead the world back to its serenity.

- **Seed Description:** Respect for each person being a creation of God.

- **Soil:** Plant this into relationships with all people, all races, backgrounds, classes, everywhere you go, no matter who they are.

- **Water:** Water this seed by being friendlier to people, smiling, opening doors for the elderly or someone else, lending a hand to an important cause pertaining to another race or culture outside of your own.

- **Oxygen:** Learn more about other races and cultures. Listen to the opinions and suggestions of others, this helps generate mutual respect.

- **Temperature:** Not everyone will respect you, even when you show the utmost respect for them. Unfortunately, not all people seek to be great, and certainly not all people care about others outside of their immediate circle. You will come across cold souls. These you can only pray for.

- **Light/Darkness:** Respect goes a long way and can have lifelong benefits. You never know who someone will become in the future or whether you will need that person or vice versa. Disrespect on the other hand is not acceptable on either side. Be the greatest person you can. If someone envies you and doesn't respect you for that, you must be prepared to let them go from your life.

- **Dormancy:** In times of dormancy, when it seems as if no one respects you and you feel like there's no need to respect anyone else, this is the precise moment to grow from within and renew your thinking. You must remain positive and optimistic, knowing that there are others, some near you and many around the world who truly believe in the greater good of all people.

- **Germination:** Support its growth by putting yourself in positions to respect someone that you'd rather not, while keeping an open mind that this is to expand your character as well. Challenges are always opportunities to grow in any area of life. Don't be phony when it comes to respect. Don't say one thing in front of people and do another behind their back, this will kill the seed and burn the soil to where it cannot be used again without forgiveness, which is not guaranteed unless a new season approaches in the heart of the forgiver.

Portland, Oregon
United States of America

"Seeing the divine intelligence in the everyday and the extraordinary capacity of the human spirit when inspired by love – to me, this is where greatness begins."

-Pat Johnson

Brand and Business Strategist

Botswana

"There is no template to being great, the greatest of us all didn't do it by being liked by everyone else, they did it by being themselves and then taking their unique brand of "them" to great extents. You cannot be great while trying to be someone else, because in you was deposited something that can change the world. Something that only you can do as you are. And that's often the hardest thing... embracing yourself and allowing that embrace to remain until the end."

-Nicolette Chinomona

Business Writer at Public New Hub

Nashville, Tennessee

United States of America

"Greatness to me means accomplishing something whether big or small that serves a purpose in enlightening or helping someone's life. I do one thing everyday to make someone's life happier...say hello to a stranger, help an older person through a door way, let a mother with children ahead of me in a grocery store line etc... My hope is that someday, through my music I can send the same positive message."

-Scott Wesley

Songwriter | Singer | Performer

BE GREAT.

Everyone would continue if they saw the finish line in front of them. When that line is nowhere in sight for days, hours, months or even years, only those who have sacrificed tremendously and prepared diligently will remain to complete the race.

Barcelona
Spain

"I think Greatness has more to do with quotidian heroism that many people show in taking care of others than with memorable exploits. There can not be Greatness in the egotism, because it does not allow anything to grow around it."

-Maria Causadias

Translator

Wichita, Kansas
United States of America

"Greatness is when others desire to follow your lead through your example. No deception, no ulterior motive. The vision, the mission, the example, the inspiration and the execution."

-Alan G. Badgley

Business Strategist/Consultant
President Global Habitat Solutions

Island of Malta

*"Can timely opportunities, careful research, step by step
preparation, or sacrifice alone help you achieve greatness?
Networking is the key seed; success that can be shared
with others!"*

-Liz Apap

Property Consultant

8:35pm - Time to be Great.

Omaha, Nebraska

United States of America

"Greatness is both illusive and elusive. It is illusive in that many seek it, like its cousin fame, for itself. It is elusive in that it cannot be sought directly, but is bestowed as a result of a lifetime of developing outstanding achievements and character. True greatness is thus not an end, but a by-product, and the truly great are most often the truly humble."

-Rodney Ruff

Writer | Editor

Seed 4
LET IT GO

LET IT GO

$\mathscr{Let}$ it go. I know it hurt you, it damaged you and it made you very sad. You felt crushed and the pain has turned into anger or hatred. Today is your day to flush the resentment from past hurt away. You have to release these impurities out of the remarkably created instrument of flesh that you live within. The human body must remain as pure as possible to operate in supreme health. My advice for you is to simply get over it. Take it to the trash, place it inside, cover it up then walk away. Don't look back and never reclaim what you've discarded. Start fresh by allowing only progressive, inspirational, and healthy thoughts and acquaintances into your life. Time will help you heal and forgive but you have to start now, today. The longer you harbor emotional and soul impurities, the faster they will spread throughout your bloodstream, turn into disease, and take you to an early grave.

- **Seed Description:** Letting go of past pain.

- **Soil:** Plant this into any area of your life that has caused you hurt, turmoil, agony, depression and/or heartache.

- **Water:** Water this by accepting the apologies of others and making peace with those you have unresolved issues with.

- **Oxygen:** Ask others who have successfully dealt with and overcome some of the same things you are dealing with to give you their coping, recovery and resilience advice.

- **Temperature:** In the heat of the moment, especially after being bruised emotionally, the last thing you want to hear someone say is "let it go" or "get over it". This is understandable. It takes time to calm down and return to some sort of peace so that rationale thinking resumes. Take some time, not too much, but just enough to analyze the situation, cry it out if you have to, then pull yourself together. The seasons of life are way too short to take more time than needed to let it go.

- **Light/Darkness:** Don't try to do it all alone. Good friends and family or even a support group can be a great asset and comfort to help you get over this rocky place in your life. Being alone is good for solitude, for thinking things through, meditation and prayer only. Surround yourself with people of light, progress and joy, those who will encourage you, motivate you, and who you know will make you smile.

- **Dormancy:** Some people struggle more than others to leave the trash in the can where it belongs. Resentment haunts the lives of so many, causing them to live in mental and emotional cages forever. There's nothing sadder in life than a broken heart that was never mended back together. When you find it hard to let go, keep in mind that your life was not created for that one situation or for that one person. This means that there's more for you to focus on and you can't let one thing ruin your entire life. You are greater and now you are wiser. Let it go, keep living.

- **Germination:** Support its growth by looking at life and experiences differently. We are all on a journey but it's up to us how we let our individual journey effect and define us. We're all imperfect people as well, so this should let you know that people will make mistakes, things will happen that we never thought would or could, lies will be told, disappointments are inevitable. Knowing this, we must prepare to not only be better for ourselves but also to challenge others to do the same, so that situations that hurt us, especially those caused by another individual, can be minimized amongst the human race. We must grow through the pain, letting the process make us and others stronger.

Newport News, Virginia
United States of America

"Greatness is intrinsic; it cannot be acquired, it can only be developed. Everyone has the opportunity to experience greatness if they humble themselves enough to acknowledge their flaws, seek purposed guidance and believe in a future that is greater than their singular existence."

-Venita N. Taylor

CEO Tailoring Dreams

Buenos Aires

Argentina

"Greatness is to be recognized as an exceptional person that can extract the most exceptional skills out of ordinary people, by acting as a guide to follow and a hero to remember."

-Rodrigo Borgia

CEO 5mol

Fairfield County, Connecticut
United States of America

"Greatness is the ability to conquer the lesser you in you so the greater you can emerge."

-Whitni Dicker

Designer Plenitude Design Group

South Africa

"Greatness is the ability to successfully share opportunities with others and create life changing differences to the benefit of all. To give someone an opportunity in life is one of the greatest gifts one can give. It takes greatness, resolve & patience to do this."

-Leon de Wet

Owner Tartra Technologies

BE BOLD.

Greatness is always expanding, even when you've mastered certain things, greatness looks for something new.

Milwaukee, Wisconsin
United States of America

"Greatness is: 1. To be true to myself by being a student/teacher, working hard to practice continuous improvement and shared learning. 2. To strive every day not to cause anyone pain. 3. To work hard on insuring my actions speak louder than my words and that I am a good model for my children and grandchildren by making a difference in the world. 4. To give more value than I receive. 5. To be humble, kind, loving, grateful and to serve/help those who are most vulnerable and in most need."

-Gregory Stromberb

CEO/Founder at Cannedwater4kids, Inc

Aydin

Turkey

"The Seed Greatness, is the ability to feel, then see, desire, dream and believe with passion what others do not, the ability to then share that passion, desire, feeling or Dream, with those around you. Then the Leadership that lies in everyone is to help those around to see what you have found which should be a benefit to mankind."

-Volkan Mahmut

Route2Turkey, Turkish Property Investment Guide

Los Angeles, California

United States of America

"Greatness is the ability to let go and allow the universe and your spirituality to guide and work through you. Greatness is knowing that you are not alone and trusting your gut instincts, regardless of opinions, criticism and fear. Greatness is taking the ultimate leap of faith, sometimes against all odds. Greatness is accepting failures or disappointments as life lessons and using them as tools for growth and expansion. Greatness is understanding that you succeed by the mere fact of acting upon a thought, idea or dream without knowing the final outcome."

-Lacy Darryl Phillips aka "Uncle Earl"

Producer/Host/DJ at The Ultimate Underground Experience
Radio Show

Seed 5

BE AUTHENTIC

BE AUTHENTIC

Your looks, your voice. Your abilities. Your likes. Your dislikes. Your ideas. All of these make up something quite spectacular, and that spectacular something is you. I find it frustrating to witness thousands if not millions of people trying to be like someone else. Did you know that everyone in the entire world has a different fingerprint? We sure do. God created you to be only you, making it impossible for a 100% complete duplication. Therefore take pride in who you are, where you're going, and what you stand for. Be authentic in your life's presentation. This means live each day as an individual contributor to the world as a whole. Share the natural ingredients that make up the main course of your soul. As a human being, you are your most powerful when you identify your natural self and learn to love every ounce of it.

- **Seed Description:** Be yourself.

- **Soil:** Plant this into everyday life decisions that you make.

- **Water:** Water it by making decisions and choices for you, regardless of the influence of others or because of what's popular.

- **Oxygen:** Take a closer look at the lives of those who you know live successfully just by being themselves and living from within. Let them inspire you to do the same, not to copy them, but to be bold enough to be the real you and listen to your own inner voice.

- **Temperature:** Being authentic, natural, doing things on your own terms, it all sounds good, but it's not an easy task. It takes courage to love yourself and it takes multiple seasons of learning and awareness to truly live from within. You must first know who you are, so start an internal investigation.

- **Light/Darkness:** Most people admire those who are authentic, those who stand on their own and express themselves naturally. Let the admiration strengthen you to enhance your authenticity for more to see. Unfortunately, most is not all, so don't expect to be celebrated by the masses just because you can make a decision based on what you want. No matter the case, be observant of your surroundings. Know when to share and be authentic to the extreme, and also know when it's better to just be present and observe.

- **Dormancy:** There will be days when you feel like being yourself may not be the best decision. Honestly, being you won't always be received well. Sometimes being authentic will isolate you, cause others to mock and scorn you, and make you want to blend in with the rest of the crowd, just so you can feel included. Don't do it. This reaction from others is quite normal. It's been that way for centuries. The norm knows and understands the norm, so whenever you stand out, their reaction to you only confirms that you are unique. Look it at that way and continue.

- **Germination:** Grow your authenticity by expressing yourself, sharing your thought-out opinions and giving of your unique skills, ideas, and talents in situations that need someone as fresh, masterful and innovative as you. Be proud that you bring new life to the table. The world needs more leaders, more thinkers and more doers. This is your opportunity to not only be yourself but to also be great.

Atlanta, Georgia

United States of America

"Greatness is the ability to find joy and peace in the many conflicts of your life, within business and social responsibility. Being at peace and giving first; greatness is viewed in you from the many friends, family and business relationships provided by giving. Support your network of family, friends and business associates and you are great!"

-Jim Browning

CEO & Chief Profit Generator at YPN Companies, Inc.

Poland

"Greatness is the courage to make decisions, take responsibility and live with the consequences."

-Krzysztof Dykas

Creative Director at New Amsterdam

Houston, Texas

United States of America

"Greatness is a hidden treasure buried in the hearts of man. Only when it has been discovered by the constant refining of failure, will it fully mature into a greatness that is incomprehensible."

-Dr. Aletha Warren

CEO VIP Access Granted

Beijing
China

"Greatness is to keep breaking the limits of your thinking. Make this life as possible as you can."

-Donghui Su

Researcher

BE WISE.

Greatness is full of surprises and can sometimes manifest in the lives of others much later, even years after your life has made an impact on them. You never know who someone will become from what you did for them, said to them or how they perceived you.

Minneapolis, Minnesota
United States of America

"Greatness is being true to yourself and others, never sacrificing your authenticity in either direction. Doing so requires a deep self-awareness, a knack for understanding others, keen powers of observation, the courage to speak up in the name of truth and all the while modeling such traits to build the courage in others to be great, as well."

-Lisa Mauri Thomas

Mauri LLC

Zambia

"For me greatness is about starting something that does not end with you. It's about realizing the fact that we did not inherit this moment from our ancestors, but that rather we have borrowed it from our descendants."

-Jordan Siame, Jr.

Partner Envirolution Consulting

Washington, DC

United States of America

"Greatness means being successful in a way that touches a lot of other people. I believe you need to start your pursuit of greatness with a worthy ideal. If your ideal is not worthy (for example, just getting rich), you are not a success by this standard even if you achieve wealth. The good news is that you can be a success just by making progress toward your ideal, even if you stumble along the way. My worthy ideal is passionate solidarity among people across religions and cultures."

-Katherine M Metres

Writer Services | Entrepreneur

Seed 6
DREAM

DREAM

Why limit yourself? A human life with limits is worse than living as a caged animal. You're surrounded by restrictions. You can't maneuver very far because you've been confined to a particular place that has become familiar, day in and day out. This is the life of millions of people around the world. Stop the madness, the drudgery, the complacency. Dream into your life! We were all born with dreams and desires. There is no reason why you shouldn't dream. It doesn't matter if you weren't born into a rich family or if you feel inadequate because someone does something better than you can. Dreams are not competitive, they are complete per person. Only you can dream your dreams. Let them birth within you so that they can breathe. This allows you to exhale them into the atmosphere. Though you may not be conscious of it, you're releasing what you desire. By remaining steadfast, prepared and focused, opportunities will open up for you, attracting to you whatever you release. When this happens, grab hold and run with it. You can do it!

- **Seed Description:** Dream

- **Soil:** Plant this into every moment you have available to look and reach within yourself to discover what it is you were born to do.

- **Water:** Water this by preparation and researching that which you dream to do or become. It's essential to becoming great at anything you desire in this area.

- **Oxygen:** Surround yourself with not only others who dream but around those who are pursuing theirs as well as those who have accomplished their dreams also. It is true that you become what you surround yourself with, very true.

- **Temperature:** Dreamers are far and wide nowadays. It seems that most people only desire to get a job and survive. This is the era we now live in, however you must only accept to live in the atmosphere of possibilities. Yes, the majority would rather not even discuss their dreams that they once had but you must stay focused no matter what the majority believes or promotes. Greatness is also the ability to decide to go against the majority.

- **Light/Darkness:** Dreamers are few, visionaries are even fewer. Isolation is expected, loneliness can be counted upon and doubts will be many, but know that this comes with the territory and life of a dreamer. On the flip side, the passion that fuels your dreams can start a flame around the world. There is nothing more amazing than an individual who dreams and inspires others to do the same.

- **Dormancy:** Dreams don't come with baking instructions or a time frame to be done. Honestly, they can be more uncertain than anything else in your life. In times of dormancy, continue to prepare and strategize ways to bring them to pass. Most of our dreams never come to life not because of a lack of money or due to a geographical location, they remain unrealized because we haven't researched, planned, networked and sat down long enough to create a concise strategy to make them come to life.

- **Germination:** Support its growth by pushing yourself beyond your own human limits to bring your dreams to pass. Studying those who are living dreams similar to yours can also inspire you into the next level. Keep an eye and ear open for opportunities related to your dreams. Take strategic risks when you see them. After you analyze the situation or opportunity and it looks worth it, give your all to making something great come out of it. Motivate others to dream into their life as well, this will always expand your spirit and cause new doors to open for you.

10:41pm - Time to be Great.

Charlotte, North Carolina
United States of America

"That unique fiber of your being that is oblivious to defeat or failure against all odds is where you'll find the gates of Greatness....only thru perseverance and determination will you pass through."

-Tom Bartlett

Actor | Singer - Professional Elvis Presley Impersonator

Bangladesh

"Greatness is doing good deeds for others."

-Mostafizur Rahman

Manager Engineering at Libra Infusions Limited

Louisville, Kentucky
United States of America

"Greatness is achieved when one comes alive with inspired thought and acts upon it despite fears, doubts or reasonable reactions - and others, no matter how few or how small or how many generations after you these others may come, are blessed by one's actions with beauty, Truth, freedom or love."

-Lin Schussler-Williams

Inspirational Speaker/Transformational Coach

BE GREAT.

The more you rely on that which is within to guide you, the more you'll realize how many people around you are not doing the same.

Karlstad
Sweden

"Greatness to me is deeper awareness in life, reached from experience and analytical thinking. Greatness and wisdom, I think, is nearly the same."

-Lisa Mattsson

Visionary

8:15am - Time to be Great.

Cedar Rapids, Iowa
United States of America

"Greatness to me is feeling comfortable in your own shoes and knowing where you stand in the world and having the power to create your own life. Stumbling blocks may occur as we walk the road that we call life. As long we have faith as well as hope within ourselves, there will be no wrong. Every action has a consequence, its goal is to move you into a positive direction to get you one step closer to achieving True Greatness and success. The sun may go down but it never forgets to shine again."

-Antonio Morales

Actor | Comedian

Albania

"Greatness is the ability to create ideas that bring people together to develop something bigger than you."

-Artur Allkoci

Owner Image Systems shpk

4:12pm - Time to be Great.

St. Louis, Missouri
United States of America

"Greatness is looking up and never seeing a ceiling."

-Mark Sanders

Director of Business Development at LockerDome

Seed 7

INSPIRATION

INSPIRATION

Are you inspired right now? You should be. We should aim to be self-inspired or inspired by something or someone else daily. Why? Because inspiration is power and comfort. Feeling empowered and comforted every single day is a must to stay above the worries and frustrations of life. If there are dozens of things aiming to bring you down on any given day, wouldn't it make sense to have at least one moment of inspiration? So many things can translate into inspiration; music, kids, exercise, movies, books, God, accolades, friends, jobs, even food for some. Take advantage of the realm of inspiration. Look for it, produce it and give it away to others once you've mastered it for yourself. Inspiration never dies, instead, it saves lives.

- **Seed Description:** The necessity of Inspiration.

- **Soil:** Find a moment to plant this into your daily life in some way. It is mandatory for the times we live in.

- **Water:** Water it by continuously looking for ways to be inspired.

- **Oxygen:** Fill your life with things and people who operate in the inspiration realm, those who love to listen to motivational messages, read inspirational writings and keep themselves encouraged throughout the week.

- **Temperature:** Inspiration is contagious. The more inspired you are, the more fired up you will be about your life, your pursuits and helping those around you feel the same. It fuels your passion. Be mindful of its power and the benefits of staying in this realm.

- **Light/Darkness:** Society doesn't publicize inspiration, instead it glorifies the complete opposite, anything and everything else that silently pounds on the conscious of our minds, creating sadness, uncertainty and doubt. Our nightly news alone can create a heavy darkness over us before we go to bed. Know that you have a choice to refuse to listen and to refuse to watch. Be mindful of what you let into your internal operating system. It will effect you in some way, sooner or later.

- **Dormancy:** What do you do when you don't feel inspired? When don't feel like being encouraged, motivated or optimistic? Well, you dance. It may sound strange but there is energy and forces within music that really does change the atmosphere. This has been known throughout centuries. It doesn't matter if you think you know how to dance or not, just move to the groove. Find some of your favorite songs, take a break to listen, sing if you want, and dance. It works for me. Music opens up an atmosphere that we can't always reach unless we hear music itself. If that doesn't work for you, go to a mirror, look at yourself and declare that even though you may feel down right now, it is only for this short moment. You may need to lay down, take a nap and regroup. This is normal, don't feel bad about it. Inspiration can drain you physically just as much as it can empower you spiritually. So rest, listen to a few tunes if you have to. Once you feel some of your power returning, use that to push yourself back into high gear. This is mindset of the greats and of champions.

- **Germination:** Support its growth by creating inspirational environments to enter when you need it most. Keep a book handy or a quote, a scripture or anything that makes you want to ascend to a higher conscious and think more positive. There's more than enough aiming to bring you down daily, I say this time and time again, so use everything you've got to maintain the highest level of inspiration on a daily basis.

Scottsdale, Arizona

United States of America

"What greatness means to me? It's simple, it means to focus on the best everyday, to do your best and always expect the best. When you do these three things greatness always comes to you in return."

-Tom Ziebell

CEO Ziebell Holdings

Brussels
Belgium

"To me, greatness is the destination of an inner journey, the one that will uncover all my weaknesses, fears, strengths and potentialities; building acceptance for the former and achievements from the later. It is about accepting past failures as the seeds for future successes. It is about rising to peace and freedom of mind, as a reward for never giving up on a long and sometimes chaotic journey. It is about paving the way for the generations to come, as a beacon provides reference and confidence to sailors on a misty sea."

-Jean-Cedric Bienfait

Solution Architect Information Management at Altran

Indianapolis, Indiana

United States of America

"Greatness is the ability to persevere in the face of adversity. Not settling for the "status quo" but having the tenacity to move in a positive direction with stability, creativity, compassion & excellence."

-Shaylae Duprís

Human Resources

Oslo

Norway

"Greatness happens when great words are followed by great action."

-Andreas Ursin Hellebust

Film Producer at Oslofilm AS

BE BOLD.

We must accept that we were built to withstand all kinds of turmoil and sadness. We are overcomers by heart and resilient by spirit.

Denver, Colorado
United States of America

"Greatness to me means the capacity and ability to extend love to others in all situations. Love encompasses all the truly great qualities of a person."

-Scott Smeester

Revenue Generation Engineer

Sydney
Australia

"Greatness is being present to your authentic self, loving and accepting all of who you are, embracing your darkness as much as your light, and showing up in the world living your truth. It's believing that wishes do come true and realizing how powerful you really are."

-Anfernee Chansamooth

Australia's #1 Confidence Coach

New York, New York

United States of America

"Greatness is not a privilege, nor a happenstance or technicality; it's not some inevitable seed waiting to happen. Greatness is your God-given right, but she will not know you unless you claim her in season proper."

-Jermyn Shannon EL

E-Business | Startup Consultant | Digipreneur

Seed 8

OPPORTUNITY

OPPORTUNITY

Don't just "seize the day". You have the power to create the entire day that you want to seize. Every morning presents itself as formless clay. You must become the potter and designer of what you'd like to see. Tomorrow's work of art, meaning the things you want to manifest in your life, depends on how you mold and knead your 'day clay' today. Understand that you have more control over directing your future than you perceive. If you want happiness, make it mandatory to mold happiness into your day clay. Discover what gives you that happy feeling then add it in. And this goes for everything else you desire. Recognizing the 'gift of opportunity' is the starting line for a life of fulfillment. After you recognize it, you have no excuses for not pursuing what you want out of life. When you wake up and say to yourself "I will figure out a way to make this happen or to make this better", then you've entered the opportunity realm. So instead of just seizing the days that come, enter the realm of opportunity and start creating those days you want to seize.

- **Seed Description:** Creating opportunities.

- **Soil:** Plant this into your daily, weekly, monthly, annually and long-term planning.

- **Water:** Water this seed by deciding what it is you want out of life, if not everyday then at least every year. Write it down so you can see it and read over it to remind yourself that you need to be pursuing it constantly. This is not the same as a New Year's resolution. This must become a life choice, a life change, a mindset alteration.

- **Oxygen:** Start setting things in place beforehand so that you can get expected results quickly, soon, or in the long run. For example, if you know you need to learn specific information before a meeting or job interview, then make sure you get it done, in addition to extra research so you'll stand out amongst your colleagues or other applicants. You'll be more impressive and aware because you created and took additional steps to seize the opportunity.

- **Temperature:** There are seasons for everything, including opportunities. Your job is to remain alert through observation and instinct, to recognize when it's too cold to strike or when the perfect time arrives to snatch it up.

- **Light/Darkness:** To live in the realm of opportunity can be lonely. Not everyone will be as optimistic as you are but you must continue. On the other hand, connecting with those who operate in this realm can prove extremely beneficial. People who live in this realm will gladly share and seek to create other opportunities with you.

- **Dormancy:** As long as you awake each day, opportunities will be available in some shape, form or fashion. They are rarely completely dormant because each day was created to present plenty of opportunities, depending all on your perception. If you so happen to feel a sense of dormancy, then the next step is to create an opportunity. Opportunities are only dormant if you don't participate in daily life.

- **Germination:** Support the growth of opportunities by expanding your knowledge of everything, not just things you want to know but also about things you never had an interest in. The more exposure, information, and education you can obtain, the more opportunities will make themselves known. Opportunities are endless, they have no measure and they are active every waking moment of your life if you focus on them.

Little Rock, Arkansas
United States of America

"Greatness is the heartbeat of Service."

-Bernice Angoh

Author | Speaker

Founder The Forever Young Revolution and L.I.F.E

Bratislava

Slovak Republic

"You can not describe Greatness by words. Greatness is to be seen, touched, heard or felt. People will use different words to describe it, but feeling is the same. It is the awe which you feel while being in the presence of Greatness itself. No matter where, whether giving standing ovation for a talented person at a concert or at an X-factor show, or after seeing a great movie after which you can not simply move or after successfully passing the toughest exam of your life. No matter where and when, for you time just stopped and you feel Greatness. This Greatness inspires you to see beyond any limits and allows you to realize that Greatness is reachable even by yourself."

-Martin David

State Advisor of the Government Office

Los Angeles, California

United States of America

*"Greatness is climbing up the ladder never looking back.
Once you reach the top then you can look down to reach out
a hand and pull someone up."*

-Dennis Robinson

CEO Dennis Robinson Personal Training

Celebrity Trainer

BE WISE.

Look at life as most films are produced, creating from the end to the beginning so you'll know exactly what you're aiming for as far as the finished product.

Kiribati

"Greatness is humbleness and sacrifices intentionally instigated and offered by any person to ultimately let the goodness diffuse across communities and nations. Greatness is not about climbing up to reach the top of a ladder, but it is you being at the bottom holding the ladder to let everyone else climb up. Those who reach the top of a ladder will not be of greatness until they hold another ladder for others to climb. Making sacrifices with an untainted heart and mind for others to live, for others to be happy, for others to stop suffering, for others to be cured, for others to be loved should be the basis for greatness. To me, learning to humble myself and make sacrifices at all costs is learning to achieve greatness."

-Buriata Eti Tofinga

PhD Student at University of the South Pacific

Fort Lauderdale, Florida
United States of America

"Greatness if the ability to save lives."

-David Pressler

President at DRD Enterprises Inc.

Bahrain

"Greatness to me is a man's attitude in the face of everything - a smile in the face of adversity; composure in times of extreme joy; presence and peace of mind when under pressure; a strong shoulder to others in times of need. It's thankfulness to the Almighty under every circumstance."

-Abdulaziz Khattak

Sub Editor/Reporter at Gulf Construction Magazine

Baltimore, Maryland
United States of America

"Greatness comes about through hard work and the pursuit of one's goals, and the experiences you encounter along the way. Making a difference in people's lives, being rewarded, and acknowledged by your peers and those you interact with in daily life, is TOTAL EUPHORIA...."

-Gwen Stevenson

Hospitality Professional & Business Owner

Seed 9

SACRIFICE

SACRIFICE

Lose your title. Silence your ego. Put your wants aside for now.

There are times in life when we must work without recognition, cry without comfort, stand in the gap when it seems like no one else will, and encourage others though the favor isn't returned. Don't let sacrifice sadden or depress you. The purpose of sacrifice is to humble you and help you remain teachable. It cleanses you, giving you new eyes that allow you to see things, people, and life more clearly. Sacrifice builds character and integrity while preparing you for divine promotion. God sees your sacrifice and He rewards your obedience. Lift up your head during your process of sacrifice. What you carry within you is greater than any sacrifice. You are a carrier of humility, long-suffering, strength and grace. Share it with this world in need.

- **Seed Description:** Sacrifice

- **Soil:** Plant this into your goals, dreams, pursuits, responsibilities to yourself and to others.

- **Water:** Water it by giving of yourself to others when they need help or encouragement. Also by always keeping your focus on the big picture while you sacrifice for your long-term goals.

- **Oxygen:** Notice the sacrifice of others who give of their time, talent, and even their finances often. Let this motivate you. Study those before you who made huge sacrifices to get to where they are in life or to achieve what they've accomplished. Let this produce hope and perseverance in you.

- **Temperature:** Sacrifice isn't pretty when it comes to greatness. It takes a very tenacious individual to endure to the end in spite of all the uncertain obstacles and difficulties that could present themselves. It can lead you to your boiling point if you aren't constantly aware of the purpose of the sacrifice. Remain focused on your goal. When sacrificing for others, this should be rewarding to the heart and uplifting like a fresh breeze. Helping others and knowing that your presence matters in their life should always encourage you to want to do more.

- **Light/Darkness:** You must continue to inspire yourself in times of great sacrifice. The process alone can be draining, stressful and discouraging. You will some high days and some low days. On the low days, have a backup plan to bring yourself back to the high place, some type of inspiration or motivation waiting to be activated to keep you out of the slumps as you endure the sacrifice.

- **Dormancy:** There are days when you may feel like your sacrifice is in vain. You will feel as though no matter how much you sacrifice, nothing will ever change or that the mission will never be accomplished. To this I say continue.

To be great, you continue regardless. We'll never know the answers until we reach the place to find them. You'll never get there if you quit. True enough, nothing in life is guaranteed, but I guarantee if you don't pursue something, you are guaranteed nothing.

- **Germination:** Support its growth by the mere fact that it has to be done. This you must accept deep down within you. We all make sacrifices, whether it's for family, career, goals, whatever the case, sacrifice is a part of life. You must program your mind to this fact. It must be done in order for you to experience your own inner and outer power, also to build your character, integrity, patience and your ability to persevere. This is essential for greatness. It cannot be overlooked and you will not be able to 'skip to the next step'.

New Orleans, Louisiana
United States of America

"Greatness to me means moving with the favor that I have, with a tenacity that has no other manifestation other than the ultimate success that it brings, with an absence of arrogance and presence of humility to simply prove and glorifying that God is. It means I'm blessed with wisdom to be able to teach and I have the love of Jesus that assures my salvation in the course of God's Grace that has sustained me. God's greatness validates my role and my purpose, therefore, I produce!"

-Glenn A. Broom

VP-Planning & Development at Nolatown, Inc.

San Jose

Costa Rica

"Greatness is our natural, internal ability to find the way to become the best version of us, on every single act of compassion, on every single act of love, understanding and courage. But Greatness is also a path, a road full of discipline, hard work, knowledge and a lot of fun!"

-Marco Astúa

CEO aPlicativa | Software Entrepreneur

Union County, New Jersey

United States of America

"Greatness is measured by your gifts, passion, hard work and determination. Greatness is overcoming the odds, the negativity and doing something that a hater says you can't achieve and especially overcoming all the challenges. That means to overcome your fear, obstacles. Have no fear and live up to the greatness."

-Joanel Simelus

Internet Visionary

Business Development at Family Price Book

Slovenia

"Greatness is about becoming your best self and putting lifetime smiles not on people's faces, but in their hearts. It's about being better everyday and helping everything that surrounds you to grow. Be it your family, the company your work in, the team you lead, the organization you manage, your local community, your country, your world. It's not about being perfect, but it's about leaving this world a little better than it was."

-Rok Snoj

Entrepreneur

BE GREAT.

There are seasons when change must be silent and wait. During these moments we should prepare for a greater return, a mightier rush, your most powerful flow. Greatness should always increase.

Atlanta, Georgia
United States of America

"Great people don't just believe great things, or plan great things, or affirm great things. They take action and they achieve great things. All people are valuable because of their potential, but some people will become great because of their actions. Action is the path to greatness because it makes impossible things possible and turns "could" into "did." Greatness, therefore, is the fruit of action intensely and incessantly applied to the realization of a core value."

-Joe M. Turner

Chief Impossibility Officer at Turner Magic & Keynotes

Sao Paulo

BRAZIL

"Man's greatness resides in his constant desire to know the world around him and to know himself."

-Luiz Bittencourt

Experienced IT Manager

Upper Darby, Pennsylvania
United States of America

"In my opinion, greatness is the power we all have in us to impact our own lives and the lives of those around us. This power can be used to be an asset or a liability. It is up to each individual to decide how we use this power that we are born with. Personally, I choose to use this power to inspire, encourage and uplift those around me. This in turn enables them to use their power to overcome the obstacles they encounter in life."

-Katrina Brittingham

Owner and Readiness Consultant VentureReady, LLC

Seed 10

TAKE CHARGE

TAKE CHARGE

What are you waiting for? It seems as though everyone is

waiting on something or waiting on someone to do something for them. Divine positions that you'll be placed in during life have little to do with skills or ability. Instead, it all revolves around your passion and willingness to learn with each circumstance. Therefore, stand up and take your position. Unlock any limits you allowed yourself or the world to place on you. You are the CEO of your life. You are responsible for making the rules, developing the right strategies, and determining what best fits the big picture. Having the take charge attitude will automatically open up leadership platforms and abundant advancement opportunities for you.

- **Seed Description:** Take charge of your life with boldness.

- **Soil:** Plant this into your daily decisions and long-term planning, letting it empower you to have the greatest influence in how your life, dreams and goals are pursued and guided.

- **Water:** Water this seed by stepping up to the leader in situations where no one else wants the responsibility.

- **Oxygen:** Encourage others, especially our youth, to be bolder in making quality decisions for their life, not following the trends, the in-crowd and others who may not have their best interest at heart.

- **Temperature:** You must wake up each day, carrying this seed as a torch. Several people live inefficient and passive lives, only accomplishing the average and typical, that is, what is expected of them by the masses or that which is around them. You are a person of greatness, so the way you think, speak, prepare and pursue must be elevated.

- **Light/Darkness:** Being a leader is not an easy job. It is by far one of the loneliest and self-sacrificial, but it also the most rewarding. You are responsible for what goes right and for what goes wrong. Right now, your life has the potential to change more lives than ever before. Learning to take charge and be bold throughout life is power in itself, however you can't get there overnight. It takes experience, trial & error, sacrifice, humility, hard work, and know-how.

- **Dormancy:** I have days when I don't want to lead. You will too but don't tell anybody like I just did. And these are the days when all it takes is for me to cross paths with one person that needs motivation. I automatically return to leadership mode and begin releasing words of encouragement. Taking charge and being bold are gifts, some people never open them to see what's inside. If you do open them, they not only benefit your life, but should be used strategically to empower those who need them more than you do.

- **Germination:** Support its growth by studying others who have already planted this seed in their lives. Volunteer and put yourself in positions that require you to take charge, make leadership decisions, and be bold.

Boston, Massachusetts

United States of America

"Greatness is recognizing and using the simpleness of the right attitude to affect change. It is living the attitude that a defeat is not failure but an opportunity to learn, adapt and win. It is living the attitude of gratitude and service. It is living the attitude of humility (the most misunderstood leadership quality). It is living the attitude that love heals all."

-David Allen

Founder Caledonia Construction

Bulgaria

"I feel greatness when I look in my 3 year old sons eyes, when he puts his arms around me and says - "Mom, thank you for playing with me in the puddle today! It was fun!"

-Elena Simeonova

CEO ElPrintStudio Ltd

Charleston, South Carolina
United States of America

"I feel greatness is a seed within everyone, but only those who work at cultivating the seed ever achieve it. We can all ascend to greatness in our own way if we learn from our mistakes, dare to take big risks, continue to grow our inner selves, be humble and serve our fellow man. A truly great person can put the needs of others before his own."

-Brian T. Shirley

Comedian | Author | Radio Show Host

France

"To me, greatness is a state of mind. The willingness to walk the extra mile in achieving the best for your loved ones, in committing to your company success, in supporting your country in tough times and in caring for the disabled of our society."

-Jacques-André Mayeur

Sales Director Europe/Africa Aftermarket

Algerian Branch Director at CLYDEUNION Pumps

BE BOLD.

Use curiosity to enhance your senses and knowledge of new things. This helps empower you and expand everything within you.

Seattle, Washington
United States of America

"Greatness is a process involving three simple yet effortful tasks. Step one in achieving greatness is truly knowing yourself and knowing your limits. The second step is to challenge those limits until you have exhausted all resources and surpassed even your own expectations in achieving your goal. Step three is enjoying the fruits of your labor."

-Carlton M. Withers Jr.

Armed Forces US Navy

Almaty
Kazakhstan

"Personally, greatness means to me, living a fearless life. When you are not afraid to go your own way, try and fail and not regret a thing about your past, and not think about other people's opinions. Greatness is also the ability to let it go. And of course, to love and be loved."

-Aigul Umurzakova

Marketer

Austin, Texas
United States of America

"Personal greatness comes from standing in your truth when everything and everyone around you wants to diminish you and keep you small."

-Sheree L. Ross

Filmmaker | Author

Seed 11
LISTEN WITH GOLDEN EARS

LISTEN WITH GOLDEN EARS

So many voices. So many opinions. From news stories to television, from advertisements to friends and family, so much is being said around the world everyday. Yet out of it all, what are you listening to? Or maybe, what should you be listening for? Words initiate the daily duties and operations of most of human life. They also direct the emotions, attitudes, and moods of many. In such an unpredictable world where people say things to intentionally harm one another, it's important to seek out the audible tokens of life. Times when words of inspiration, encouragement, and motivation escape from the tongue of another into the atmosphere of possibilities. This is to Listen With Golden Ears. The more tokens accumulated, the richer you become within, which then produces a token of charity to spring forth with you, allowing you to now Speak With A Ruby Tongue (reference Seed 19).

- **Seed Description:** Listen to that which encourages and uplifts.

- **Soil:** Plant this into your personal life, social life, work life, time alone, family time, television time and everyday of your life.

- **Water:** Water this seed by changing or removing what you can around you that pumps negativity into your ears.

- **Oxygen:** Find more positive speaking friends and associates, listen to motivational books on cd, tune in to more motivational television broadcasting and create an activity to verbally uplift yourself when needed the most.

- **Temperature:** In a perfect world everything and everyone around us would lend an encouraging word, smile throughout the day, and jump for joy at the thought of an opportunity to motivate someone else. Unfortunately, this is not the world we live in. Face it, you are unique and called out to be great, you wouldn't be reading this otherwise. We can't change people, we can only show them the change in us and what works for us. You will have to be wise and observant regardless, always listening, whether a situation seems good or bad, something valuable is usually present in most cases.

- **Light/Darkness:** There will be those who mock you, so be prepared for that. They don't understand the necessity to live above each day, so that you don't sway back and forth, eventually becoming uprooted from the soil, and left to die. This is not how a person of greatness lives. We seek out the best in everything and in everyone. On the other hand, you will meet like-spirited carriers of light who will encourage your walk and journey. Maintain as many great friendships as you can while you continue to listen for all things great. Call upon them when you need a few words of reassurance.

- **Dormancy:** There will be days when you don't want to hear anything and days when you wonder if anyone else is listening. This is fine for the moment, only for the moment, maybe an hour or two, unless you need a full day of rest. Take this time to rejuvenate, no phone calls, no visitors. It's obvious that your spirit may be overwhelmed. After this break, return to your place of power by communicating with those who will motivate you. Though greatness is not on a schedule, it can take a toll on the human body. It takes everything within you to operate in that constant mental, emotional and spiritual state. Greatness never rests but you must.

- **Germination:** Make it mandatory, as much as possible, to surround yourself with people and things that release positive words around you and into your life. This is the audible key to greatness. Without it, you will be locked out of inner wealth while remaining trapped into the world's fascination with poverty, drama, and dismay.

Dover, Delaware
United States of America

"Greatness is continuously achieving pre-determined goals, stabilized by life balance and purified by your values and beliefs."

-Michelle Brown-Dawson

Author | Organizational Strategist

Afghanistan

"Without any expectation, loving all humans is Greatness. Being the same in all situations of life, whether it is happiness or sorrow, that is Greatness. Without seeing GOD, believing that GOD is everywhere, that is Greatness. Taking all decisions of life from heart, not from the mind, that is Greatness. Greatness is not having everything you want, but being satisfied with what you have already."

-Mehul Sheth

Business Development Manager

Detroit, Michigan
United States of America

"Greatness is the gifts and talents God has blessed us with to bless others and make a difference. We were all uniquely and wonderfully made and there is no one else like us who can fulfill our purpose."

-Nilda G. Thomas

CEO/CMO NGT Marketing Group, LLC

BE WISE.

Observe everything, everyone, everywhere. We tend to miss out on many secrets, extraordinary occurrences and valuable wisdom during life because of our casual approach.

Croatia

"Greatness is the ability to help yourself and others by not compromising your integrity."

-Goran Radic

Managing Partner and VP Sales, Applicon

8:21pm - Time to be Great.

Milwaukee, Wisconsin
United States of America

"Greatness means overcoming obstacles in order to accomplish ones goals. The obstacles may be various life circumstances. Sometimes the obstacles may even be well-intentioned and/or ill-intentioned people. Greatness means having the determination to press forward and prevail despite these obstacles."

-Marlo Thomas

Independent OurGV Affiliate

Cairo

Egypt

"Greatness is the art of passion and determination to achieve your dream and defeating the obstacles in your way no matter how many times you fail."

-Arabian Knightz

President Arab League AllStars

Founders Arab League Records

New York, New York
United States of America

"Greatness is one who lets negativity from friends and peers fuel they're passion to succeed, those who live their passions each and everyday, those who become cheerleaders for friends and peers because their success will be yours as well. Greatness comes from God. Let God become part of your life and your prayers will be answered. No one can go it alone, so let others help you realize your goals and Greatness will follow."

-Gene Shaw

Writer | Photographer | Producer

Seed 12
EXHALE

EXHALE

$\mathcal{The}$ train behind me continued on its journey as I sat near the

water watching the birds play. I saw a sailboat passing by in the distance, moving gracefully as a painting fading away. People walked by casually, all races, shapes and sizes, noticing the rocks, water, birds, sailboats, trees, and of course the happy dogs that wanted to hang out on such a beautiful day. It seems as if we've all come to this place to seek some type of solace, peace or serenity. Day to day life isn't what it used to be.

Nowadays, it's almost mandatory to stop, wait a second, and breathe. You have to exhale before the cares of life overwhelm you. If only for an hour, or in real life for most, five minutes, take a moment to observe the natural beauty that was here before us and that will remain after us. It was all created for this purpose, to exhale and to help us return to the natural peace that only the Creator of the natural beauty can give.

- **Seed Description:** R & R, rest and rehabilitation. Also can mean rest and relaxation, rest and recuperation, rest and recreation.

- **Soil:** Plant this into stressful weeks and on days when you need it the most.

- **Water:** Life is ongoing, it only stops when we die, which means the body and the mind is always working to some capacity unless we're just couch potatoes. Knowing this, you have to water this seed by creating escapes in your life where you can have solitude, some type of refreshing and rejuvenating moment to clear your mind and notice the peace of the nature's natural beauty around you. Several take nature for granted but if you really observe it all, you'll be fascinated for the rest of your life and gain a sense of belonging to a larger picture.

- **Oxygen:** When we're at peace or in a place of solitude, our minds can think clearer, we can understand things better when there is serenity. Meditation and calming music also creates an atmosphere to help this seed breathe new life into you.

- **Temperature:** We are complex beings which could mean that some of us may have complex or even complicated lives. Still, this is no excuse not to give attention to this seed. This is mandatory. No matter how busy you think you are or how intense things are around you, there must be an open door to exhale or you will boil over right into a hospital bed before you know it. Some people use alcohol and drugs to bring them to a counterfeit atmosphere of R&R but this will never revise the soul. We are one with the creation and only by spending some time with nature or through focused observation of it, will you be able to identify this exceptional inner peace awaiting you.

- **Light/Darkness:** Taking advantage of this seed will enhance your health, your joy, your relationships and your focus in life. The downside of ignoring this seed can lead to various diseases that arise out of an overworked and overstressed life, mood swings and sleepless nights.

- **Dormancy:** There will be days when you won't be able to steal away for a moment of peace. There could be weeks and months where all you want is to be alone for 30 minutes to listen to the birds or the waves reaching the shore. There may even be years when a vacation is nowhere in sight. In times like these, you'll have to rely on the refreshing you received from your past moment of solace. Keeping in mind that you can return to this place without being there. Good thoughts can be just as powerful as being in the moment if you think of them often. Use this method until you get a chance to create another rejuvenating escape.

- **Germination:** Support its growth by constantly observing what in nature gives you peace of mind, what makes you want to stop and say "Wow, that's refreshing" or "Wow, that's breathtaking". Notice everything around you, what makes you want to relax, what makes you frustrated and makes you feel unsettled. Create your environments to cater to the inner and outer rest and rehabilitation you need so that you don't become exhausted and drained before your life accomplishments are complete.

Los Angeles, California
United States of America

"Every human being has the potential for greatness when faced with adversity or any obstacle in life. When we tap into the supernatural power from within, an outer change takes place to affect many people and increase the quality of life."

-Rachelle Love Jones

Account Executive

Fabuluxe & Co. Marketing Lifestyle Firm

5:05am - Time to be Great.

Oradea

Romania

"Up until now (age 33) I had a full life, I've co-founded and successfully sold a company to a multinational, I tried to build others and failed a lot, I had money, I had a girlfriend, I had a comfortable house, and still I wasn't happy, then I lost almost everything I had. It is just 6 months ago when I discovered what Greatness means, it was the time when I met our Lord, Jesus Christ. For me, Greatness means knowing the LOVE of God, living a life as God wishes and doing His work here on Earth."

-Flavius Saracut

Co-founder & CMO at Mobiversal

1:11am - Time to be Great.

Murdock, Florida
United States of America

"To me Greatness is accomplishing a goal that most of us overlook, happiness. Yes success is good, but success without happiness is nothing, but having both is Greatness."

-Yahaloma Ramos

Singer | Songwriter | Performer | Writer

Budapest
Hungary

"Greatness is to never to lose the desire to be "rich" and become a new person. To learn to enjoy the irony of life and to be able to inspire hope and confidence in people. To show how much is possible in life. To put our dreams into action and get together with those we really love. To accomplish a really big task and gain human respect for accomplishing that task. To know who you are and be able to inspire other peoples' emotions, their tears, and their joy. To put your whole soul into what you do, and to learn to be grateful."

-Alba Hyseni

Professional Singer | Performer

BE GREAT.

As long as the brain and mind can understand and comprehend, you must remain open to everything new it desires to store.

Memphis, Tennessee

United States of America

"Greatness is apprehended by creative ideas developed through evolution of ones self and forward thinking in motion. Ideas without action are stagnant thoughts that repel greatness. Imagination turned reality only comes to those who plant, water and nourish seeds of greatness into beauty for the eye of the beholder. A seed without water will die; an idea without development will remain dormant. Every second is a new opportunity to blaze a trail of greatness for others to lead when your memory is a legacy."

-Sherri Henley

Founder and CEO at Business Over Coffee International (BOCI)

Macedonia

"The small people enjoy the schadenfreude, the great man ignores it! Only the human schadenfreude - "Fail-Joy" makes the exception. So consequently of this, Greatness is control and rational perception of this feeling."

-Ljubomir Rogozharev

Artist | Musician

Albany, Georgia

United States of America

"Greatness to me can be summed up in nine words: Godly, Respectful, Eager, Acclaimed, Talented, Notable, Educated, Superior, and Successful."

-Tameka Kelly

Entrepreneur

Seed 13
ASK GOD

ASK GOD

What is it that worries you? What would you like to know?

Life is never spelled out for us. There is no guaranteed plan to follow. Only the designer of life knows all the answers and that designer is God. Some things can't be explained. Some things will never be defined. Knowing this, we can only turn to the source of all things, Almighty God. Ask God when your answers to life's uncertainties don't seem to add up. Ask God to show you the reason why He put you on Earth. Ask God to reveal within you the beauty of His creation, so that you can learn to become one with His masterpiece. We are limited in what we know, bias in what we feel, and unsure of how to interpret what we see. Life was never meant for us to go at it alone. From this day forward, promise me one thing, that you will always ask God.

- **Seed Description:** Ask God

- **Soil:** Plant this into everyday life, situations, circumstances and your biggest life decisions.

- **Water:** I believe that God exists, contrary to others, which is fine, everyone is entitled to their own beliefs. He alone and His creation epitomizes greatness, so water this seed by observing and researching the character of God. We are finite beings, though geniuses in our own right, from creation. Yet still there is a higher source, a higher power, a greater mind than our own. It is up to us identify this so we can enter another realm of wisdom, knowledge, understanding and peace. This is what I have learned on my journey.

- **Oxygen:** I always find it refreshing when I meet other professionals who share the same beliefs as I do. It's like we are of one mind and one spirit. God is touchy subject for most. I believe we were all created from the same entity. We're all related in some way, this I know.

- **Temperature:** We live in very intense times where many want to know "Why are bad things happening to good people?", "Where is God?", and so on. Well my friends, bad things happen to all people. We shouldn't debate and get all fired up about whether there is a God or not, we should focus on what we have in common as the human race, that which can bring us together to impact and change the world for the better.

- **Light/Darkness:** This seed can easily cause others to distance themselves from you. Not everyone appreciates an individual who relies on a relationship with God. On the bright side, this seed can also open doors that in some cases would have never opened. I say this because I've experienced many a miracles in my lifetime, around the world, that I know for a fact, 100% fact, had to do with my relationship and communication with God. I don't recommend anyone trying to push their beliefs on anyone else in any situation. I do recommend that when someone comes to you for answers or for help, that you let them know what works for you.

- **Dormancy:** I believe God answers us in a variety of ways however there are times when you will feel as if you haven't been answered. This is when you have to rely on your faith that all things will work out on your behalf. It's apparent that our Creator is beyond our comprehension so at some point in life it's best to just let that be what it is. To spend a lifetime trying to figure it all out would be useless, yielding very little results. Let God be God and you be you. No matter the problem, in the midst of times of silence when you feel no one is listening, just be still and wait. That's what I do and it always works for me.

- **Germination:** Support its growth by asking God more questions and also sharing daily things as if He didn't already know. I've learned to wake up knowing that God allowed me another day to complete this journey of life. The journey that He set before me and the journey that I'm continuing to discover. Accept your journey for what it is. Connect with others who feel the same way and those who have an internal conviction that God is leading their lives. This seed is imperative. It changes everything, has access to anything, and is limited by nothing.

Oak Park, Illinois
United States of America

"Greatness comes from within ...achieving greatness does not come from external sources. Greatness is also making sacrifices, understanding the costs and doing what others are unwilling to do, even if it's considered unpopular. Most importantly, greatness is being a shining example for others, empowering them to achieve greatness."

-Regina Dillard

CEO Go Gee! Music Publishing

Cochabamba
BOLIVIA

"Greatness, or "WOWness factor", is the power to amaze others at a level that inspires beyond normality and drags into achieving what others only dreamed about."

-Carla Doria-Medina R.

Tech Writer

Oklahoma City, Oklahoma

United States of America

"Greatness means to be satisfied in all that life has provided. To give Hope to the hopeless, to truly share the warmth of selfless love to others, to give without concern of reward, to pursue excellence without compromise, and above all else, to knowing that serving God is the most important reason to live."

-Bob Pierce

President Wiretap Telecom

BE BOLD.

Welcome boldness and endurance into your life to help you stand your ground in any unfortunate or terrifying situation.

1:32pm - Time to be Great.

Vienna
Austria

"To make More of the world, not Less. That is Greatness."

-A. C. Standen-Raz

Filmmaker, Lush Films

Minneapolis, Minnesota

United States of America

"When the energy that moves one personally forward in the world also moves the world forward as one; that is greatness."

-Mickey Mikeworth

Financial Guru and Prosperity Advocate

Montreal, Quebec
Canada

"Greatness is not acquired by showing up talents, skills or knowledge. It's not only the ability to be better than all others. It's a capacity to go further than the average, build on passions and outstanding motivations. It's the fruit of accumulated lessons of failures."

-Bruner Nozière

CEO Biznisconsult | Entrepreneur

Cleveland, Ohio
United States of America

*"Greatness means allowing a Higher-Power to use you &
your talents to serve a Higher Purpose without regard to
fortune, fame etc."*

-Wayne "Woody" Mesker

CEO Worldstock Entertainment

Seed 14
PROCESS

PROCESS

Bake a cake today and observe the necessary preparation, baking and timing procedures. After the cake is done, you've just experienced a process. Though life is not a cake, it is still created and maintained through a process. Don't try to rush your goals, dreams and desires. You can only become what you were meant to be. Moving outside of this process will only cause chaos and frustration, internally and externally. I'm not saying wait around for something to magically appear or happen in your life. Instead, prepare diligently, flow calmly and remain alert. The awareness of process itself will move you into the right direction, introduce you to the right people, open your eyes and ears to the right things at the right time, and help develop you into your ultimate self. There are no promises that this will be an easy road, there will be testing times that suggest you give up but you must stay in the oven, bake thoroughly, so that you can come out complete and perfect. Process produces perfection. Welcome it.

- **Seed Description:** Welcome process.

- **Soil:** Plant this into situations, pursuits and decisions that take longer to sort out, achieve and decide upon.

- **Water:** The best way to water process is by practicing patience because process requires more patience than anything else. Place yourself in situations where your patience can be pushed to the limit. Yes this might sound crazy but how else can you become better at anything without testing it, practicing it and growing from what you learn. This is to think great.

- **Oxygen:** Just about every successful person, every invention, every goal, every profitable business, have all experienced process. Study the process of things around you, this will encourage you to continue with your own.

- **Temperature:** In today's society process if frowned upon by the many who desire microwaveable results and solutions on a daily basis. Don't be surprised if some of these people tell you that you're wasting your time in school or that there's a faster way to get ahead in life or how to bypass a certain situation by taking the easy route. You have to decide that if you want things a certain way, if you want to be fully informed, skilled, and educated enough to maintain it afterwards, that walking through the process is the way to go.

- **Light/Darkness:** I wish I could guarantee you that all process will deliver your desired results but I can't. What I can guarantee is that your value will increase internally through each process, which places you in a much better position to deliver externally than you would have been able to if you did not go through the process at all.

- **Dormancy:** Honesty is the best policy so I have to tell you that there may be countless moments, mornings, afternoons, and nights where you won't see any results from the process. Some processes can bring you to tears and depression, but the ultimate goal is to build you from within, to make you whole, so always keep your eye on those prizes and the finished product. No one would have ever imagined that from a few eggs, added to oil, flour, sugar, baking powder, butter, salt, and so forth would produce a moist, delicious and beautiful cake creation that brings smiles to everyone it encounters. The processes in your life are not only for you but also for you to share and use to guide others in their time of process.

- **Germination:** Support its growth by taking on the challenges and long-term steps that come with life and your pursuits. Don't back down or try to take every quick route your life GPS suggests. Let process be your desire, let it create in you depth and lay the groundwork you need to be a leader. Let it remind you that anything worth having is worth putting in the work for it, and most of all, let process make you great.

Atlanta, Georgia
United States of America

"Greatness is the ability to pursue your personal vision and over a significant period of time, consistently bring creativity and innovation to your field of endeavor while also maintaining integrity without ever sacrificing your commitment to excellence."

-Vince Rogers

Principal Change Agent at Vince Rogers & Associates

Thimphu
Bhutan

"Greatness is the purity of hearts in our leaders, which provides them with the wisdom to propagate peace in the world. Greatness is the sincerity of purpose in individuals that allows them to fulfill their goals without trampling those of others."

-Om Nirola

Management Consultant

San Antonio, Texas

United States of America

"Greatness is embracing others for the benefit of the greater good. We are meant to empower others, seek out their greatness, passion and purpose. We are all different, which makes us special. Our acceptance of being special is our bond, our greatness."

-Deborah M. Oveland

FNP-BC Special Needs Education Consultant

Greece

"Greatness can be judged by the way people treat each other, how we help each other and not kill each other, and how we care for the well being of others and not only ourselves."

-Vayia Brillis

Project Manager at Innova S.A.

BE WISE.

Greatness is not a popular pursuit, which means those who pursue that realm are a part of a new and extraordinary minority. This presents its own set of issues however, creating solitude and isolation at the highest degree.

Raleigh, North Carolina
United States of America

"Greatness can be defined in numerous ways. Greatness is achieving your goal while success accompanies greatness. Being the best in your field, being considered the greatest of all time, and receiving accolades and outstanding accomplishments means you have achieved the moment of greatness you have thrived for."

-Dr. Kimberly Juanell Pettaway

CEO KOLORZ of Cancer | CEO Cor'Rae Mgmt Agency

Pakistan

"Greatness is the ability to contribute to society on a grand scale first by changing oneself and then impacting others by example and inspiration."

-Dr. Asir Ajmal

Professor of Psychology at University of Central Punjab

Santa Monica, California

United States of America

"Greatness, it is when you consciously take responsibility for other peoples' well-being."

-Sanzhar Kettebekov

Ph D, CEO Receptive

Windermere, Florida

United States of America

"Greatness is, loving like you've never been hurt, following wisdom like you've never failed, and being happy like you've never suffered. Greatness is, loving unconditionally, pursuing dream faithfully, creating value unbeatably, and living abundantly. Greatness is being a natural and united part of the Universe. Greatness is blessed in every life."

-Spring Yan Zheng

Happiness & Thought Leadership Coach

Founder of Spring Magic Life Society

Seed 15
COMMITMENT

COMMITMENT

What's the purpose of pursuing something if you're only going to give up after the first try? It's useless. There are several things related to where you want to go and who you want to be, that requires a determined and aggressive commitment until your goals are met. This isn't just a decision, it's a force within you that carries enough power to calm a raging sea. While others boast about making New Year's resolutions annually, you need to decide only to make deeply-rooted commitments that enable you to live the life you want. Commitment separates the winners from the losers, the doers from the hearers, the achievers from the observers, and the world changers from the complainers. Commit to listen to, love and respect the genius within you. Commit to follow your heart and live from within, in order to contribute your gifts and purpose to the world. Life will commit back to you and show you the right paths to take.

- **Seed Description:** Commitment

- **Soil:** Plant this into things you feel like giving up on even when you know you shouldn't.

- **Water:** Water this by dedicating your focus and time to that which requires your commitment of them both.

- **Oxygen:** Determine to see things through all the way, no matter the time commitment, sacrifice or investment, especially if you know that it's worth it in the long run.

- **Temperature:** Commitment takes sacrifice. Sacrifice requires strength, patience, and long-suffering. These are hard to come by for most people. Know that serious commitment must only be pursued by those who have boldness and a clear vision of the task or goal.

- **Light/Darkness:** Trust and believe you will often think you are the only one being totally committed in several situations. Hopefully that's not the case in a love relationship type situation. As far as your life and becoming great, commitment is high up there amongst the traits and attributes you must embody. Every leader, inventor and great mind had and has to commit to what it is they stand for, create and believe in. No matter what others say or don't say, do or don't do, let your commitment speak for you. Let it teach you, make you great and enhance your dignity.

- **Dormancy:** Sometimes we can't see the light at the end of tunnel. Sometimes there is no tunnel and no light. You will have days when you ask yourself what's the purpose of committing when everyone else does whatever they want. The answer is simple, because you desire to be greater and not like everyone else. The whole idea of commitment is to continue. If you need a break, take it. Once that is over, return to the task, to your focus, to your greatness.

- **Germination:** Support its growth by keeping in mind the importance of and the results of commitment. Several things would not be present today if someone didn't commit to them. If surgeons and doctors didn't commit to completely surgeries, several of us wouldn't be alive. If inventors didn't commit to producing prototypes and the first of some of the actual inventions we have today, our lives wouldn't be as easy or convenient. Commitment changes lives and it changes the world. Notice the commitment of others and their positive results, let this inspire you to continue on your path to greatness.

Milwaukee, Wisconsin
United States of America

"Greatness is the ability to seek, recognize, find, and appreciate greatness in the ordinary people around you."

-Neal Wooten

Author of Reternity

Prague
CZECH REPUBLIC

"Greatness is ability to be focused on one goal - give significant value to the world and change it forever."

-Radek Vacha

Enterprise Architect

New York, New York
United States of America

"The relentless search for greatness shines through every commitment, discipline and action. While consistently striving for excellence, the steps you take will ultimately define you and impact the rest of the world. It all starts with you as an individual. You make the sacrifice and investment and become completely responsible for your success. You can't blame your parents, where you were born, your environment, or your ethnicity. It is up to you on how you navigate your successful journey to greatness...stay conscience, because the world is watching you!"

-Renee Benot

CEO Jonei Productions | Woflat Capital Group

BE GREAT.

This is the evidence of greatness, to become what wasn't, what is, and to remain, never uprooted during the earthquakes of life.

Sri Lanka

"What ever happens, what ever situations, having ability to stand, believing in myself and to keep trying to achieve what I can do for others to have a better life, this is Greatness."

-Chinthaka de Silva

Consultant BizAppsi

Tampa, Florida
United States of America

"True greatness...? Being capable of compassion, humor, and humility when you're at your highest, and lowest."

-Terri Benincasa

Boomer Expert | Host of Boomer Nation! Radio Show

Korea

"Greatness is the impressive challenge of becoming who you truly are...in that place it is born."

-William B. Choi

Business Development at Cleantech

Philadelphia, Pennsylvania

United States of America

"Greatness means fulfilling your God-given purpose and making a difference in the lives of others."

-Obioma Martin

President OMART Training and Development

Seed 16
A LIVING POEM

A LIVING POEM

Each day of life is symbolic of a new line in a poem. Words and days linked together to interpret one's individual language of existence. Our life design is to be a progressive journey of experiences and ideas, becoming a full composition of many things. Build upon your days with that which inspires you, motivates you, and adds to your composition. You just might be the only hope or inspiration for a deprived soul. Never forget that there could always be someone watching you, or even closer, reading you.

- **Seed Description:** Let your life be a living example of greatness.

- **Soil:** Plant this into everyday and every moment you have the opportunity to influence anyone in a positive way.

- **Water:** We have more influence and impact on others than we realize. Most people look to others for advice, information, suggestions or someone to emulate. Water this seed by using your life and your life influence strategically. Use it to help those who need it and want it the most. Don't waste your greatness on those who don't appreciate your value.

- **Oxygen:** Breathe life into this seed by connecting with those who desire to live on a higher plateau, those like-spirited individuals who know that it's our own personal responsibility to contribute some type of assistance to the world during our lifetime.

- **Temperature:** You have to constantly remain attuned to your inner self for this seed to survive and flourish. You must watch closely so that the seasons and tests of life do not scorch your soil and burn your root.

- **Light/Darkness:** The benefit of this seed is be to filled to the rim with joy and humility within your soul, knowing that you've been a part of making someone else's journey a little or a lot better. This seed also carries a burden of loneliness because several people are afraid to plant it, thus making the crop rare and without many to refer to, count on, or encourage you.

- **Dormancy:** There will be moments, not many, only a few, when you don't want to be an example. You will feel as though you've already been stretched beyond your mental, emotional and spiritual capacity. This is normal but must not remain the norm. Never let these dormant moments turn into several days. The greatness within you can drain you if not sourced and balanced strategically. Therefore friends, you must rest and promptly return. Greatness is only granted to those who will use it, not to those who will sleep on it.

- **Germination:** Support its growth by doing things that you are passionate about, those which can also result in helping others to succeed. Just being you and showing up to support your own desires has the power to inspire the passions and desires of those around you. You have the power to impact the entire world just by showing up on one day. Greatness is full of surprises and can sometimes manifest in the lives of others much later, even years after your life has made an impact on them. You never know who someone will become from what you did for them, said to them, or how they perceived you. Be the example, someone is always watching.

Malmo
Sweden

"To me Greatness means exactly what the title says. For every right planted seed, you take one step further to your goal. You have to plant if you want to harvest."

-Ernesto Prosperi

Operations Manager

Chicago, Illinois
United States of America

"I stand in front of a mirror and wonder if I have Greatness in me? Where does it come from? I believe it comes from the random acts of kindness that I love to bestow on strangers and sometimes friends that least expect it... because it is in that moment that I feel the Greatness, that is God."

-Taireez Niswander

CEO Silvery Moon Consulting

London, England

United Kingdom

"Greatness means acknowledging how infinitely small you are in comparison to the rest of the universe."

-Hercules Fisherman

Artist | Serial Entrepreneur

Seattle, Washington
United States of America

"Greatness is having the tenacity to strive to be better person. Greatness comes in many forms and can be found in a moment of care for another, or in a lifetime of commitment for humanity. God is greatness and when we strive to be more like God we too can be great. To me, greatness is accomplishing what others see as impossible. Not listening to discouragement but rather moving forward even in the midst of difficulties and setbacks."

-Lo Rene`

Musician | Songwriter | Author | Motivational Speaker

BE BOLD.

It is important that we know what message our life is delivering to others on a daily basis.

Nepal

"Overflowing simplicity and down to earth. Spreading positive vibes among people and finding happiness in other people's happiness for me is Greatness."

-Lucky K Chhetri

Founder/Director of Empowering Women of Nepal and 3 Sisters Adventure Trekking P. Ltd.

Boston, Massachusetts
United States of America

"Greatness is the ability to do what others will not do, while they are telling you it cannot be done."

-Jacqui Senn

Motivational Speaker | Life Coach

Toronto, Ontario
Canada

"Greatness is the moment when you realize how in love you are with who you are because you do not give up on your dream. It is accepting that you define your beauty, your role and the change you make in the world."

-Ayeesha S. Kanji

Owner ASK.Solutions

Seed 17

FREE YOUR MIND

FREE YOUR MIND

$\mathscr{I}$tell you yes and yes again my friend, you must live with an

open mind. Life, our families, our communities, and the world will all serve you a plate of their own opinions and agendas. This is a part of growth that we all experience yet as you mature and validate yourself from within, it is important to keep an open mind to new things and other views. There are things that I know for sure, and I stand firm on those things. Then again, there are things I thought I knew until I was made aware of what is accurate, true or a better way to comprehend it. Life is too short to think you know it all. You will never know it all but your mental, emotional and spiritual person within needs to acknowledge it all, which in return gives you access to more people and unlimited influence. You don't have accept everything but you must be aware of it. Lack of knowledge is an insult to the Creator. Don't limit the unlimited, which is you.

- **Seed Description:** Maintain an open mind for growth.

- **Soil:** Plant this into every situation where you would normally try to avoid learning about a particular subject or try to ignore someone's opinion.

- **Water:** Water this seed by listening more to those around you. Yes, some people really don't have anything worth listening, this I sadly agree, to for those that do, take an extra moment and let them express themselves. You will often learn something new about them or yourself during these times.

- **Oxygen:** Unless you are in school, constantly researching online or reading a variety of books, it's very hard to expand your mind and intellect if those around you aren't doing the same. It is imperative to network and befriend more people that know about things you don't so that you can learn what you never knew. Not only is this a characteristic of greatness, it's also an attribute of genius. Surround yourself with people who know more than you or those who can teach you things you haven't been taught.

- **Temperature:** Take heed as you grow older to not become mentally complacent and stale. Several people stop learning altogether, even though the world continues to innovate, upgrade, and expand. We can always learn in some capacity, no matter our age. As long as the brain and mind can understand and comprehend, you must remain open to everything new it desires to store.

- **Light/Darkness:** It fascinates me how the world's richest only make up 1% of the population. That goes to show that maybe it could be possible that the majority, the other 99%, is thinking alike. This means that as you grow into your greatness, thinking higher, pursuing more, the majority may not follow you. You must push through the gate to discover more than what the lazy mind wants to work to receive. You must knock down the boundaries around of mediocre thinking, then run out and capture unlimited thinking, so that your life can resemble what is within you.

- **Dormancy:** Learning takes energy and sacrifice. You will have days where you feel like all mental energy is gone. In addition, days where you ask yourself "What's the purpose of it all?", may be more frequent than you desire. There's more than enough to know and learn, so rushing it won't make it any better. Take it all in stride, one day at a time. Greatness is not on a schedule, it arrives with you as long as you remain open-minded to its traveling requirements.

- **Germination:** Support the growth of this seed by deciding to view the world and everything in it through a wider lens. Know that we were all placed here together, therefore, we obviously have something in common. Be open-mined enough to seek out the similarities that unite us and be brave enough to share them with the entire world.

Barquisimeto

Venezuela

"Greatness is to be able to reach your full potential, rejoice and help others to reach theirs by guiding them through your experience."

-William Gonzalez

Professor of English

Lakewood Ranch, Florida

United States of America

"We all have greatness within us, we just need the right tools to help us uncover this greatness we possess. I believe greatness can be defined by each of us differently. To me, greatness is a combination of being loving, true to your core values, inspiring, believing in possibilities, seizing opportunities, believing in yourself and those around you, and doing what others are too afraid to do. I also believe that those of us who have discovered our greatness should share the love and help others discover their own greatness."

-Doug Phillips

CEO DOSH Management Inc.

Thailand

"Greatness is not seeing yourself big and everything else small. It is the ability to see everything larger than life. By being big, you overlook all the small things. By keeping yourself small, you will be able to enjoy all the beautiful details of the things that surround you. Keep humble. Keep searching. Keep learning. Now, that is greatness."

-Piyapong Muenprasertdee

Co-founder and CEO Indie Campfire

Memphis, Tennessee

United States of America

"Greatness means to tap deep into that secret place in your heart where courage lives and pull out that "thing" that keeps you connected to the world. Greatness is the ability to still stand when grief, calamity, and storms come. It's the ability to laugh into the face of what tried to kill you and say "Ha! I'm still here! I'm still here!" When you can do that, you have reached greatness."

-Lisa Mason Minter

Independent Distributor at It Works! Global

BE WISE.

The purpose of sacrifice is to humble you and help you remain teachable.

Mexico

"Greatness is to transcend and leave a legacy, is helping others to transform their lives in positive ways, is to grow from our mistakes being humble, is being eager to learn and share our knowledge."

-Rodolfo Vega

CEO Synergy Studio | CEO Nacional de Héroes

Irving, California
United States of America

"Greatness is found in embracing humility. The moment we accept our own limitations and acknowledge God's power in our weakness, is the same moment greatness is achieved."

-Michelle Rice

Director of Sales, Zther

Asuncion

Paraguay

"Greatness is to assume the power we have to improve the lives of others."

-Carla Cassanello

CMO Install This App

Seed 18
LIFE OBSERVATION

LIFE OBSERVATION

Cherish moments. Stop, look at the trees, smile at the birds, open a door for someone. We've gotten so far from our serene place inside. That place of peace and love, where all becomes one around you. People now use everything possible to return to that realm of neutrality. It's easy to let this life pass by without ever meeting life itself. The grass will grow, the sun will set, the leaves will fall, and you will end your life without a smile if you never stop, even for thirty seconds, to see the bird in the tree. Responsibilities are a part of life. They can also produce bad stress, which produces sickness, which can produce pre-mature death. You have the power to make yourself important to you. You must celebrate your moments. How can we ever take care of others when we barely take care of ourselves. No, don't stop your life, instead, enhance your life by engaging life from within, observing all things in a more optimistic light, using each day as a learning experience to grow and explore while living in your moments, not letting them pass you by. Observe, participate and let life live through you. Be careful not to let your to-do list replace your to-live list.

- **Seed Description:** Observe yourself and your world to live greater.

- **Soil:** Plant this into every moment of life. We often go from day to day not learning much, just duplicating the same cycles, interacting with the same people and ending the day with the same results. Observe and learn more than what is expected or scheduled.

- **Water:** Water this seed by acknowledging great things about yourself that you like or do well. Celebrate your accomplishments. You can fully appreciate other's when you truly appreciate your own.

- **Oxygen:** Share the importance of thinking outside the box and participating in life, especially during moments where we don't feel like it. Let family members, friends and co-workers know that there is more to experience, more to obtain and more to explore. Too often we want this and that to change or be better yet we continue to repeat our same routine every single day.

- **Temperature:** This seed is like a whale in the ocean compared to the smaller fish. The smaller fish outnumber the whales by far. This means that most people you meet do not think or operate on this level of life, so don't be surprised if you are misunderstood, ignored or outnumbered.

- **Light/Darkness:** This seed allows you to not only see your life through more clearer but also reveals the problems and disturbances that many face. This is where greatness steps up and moves toward creating solutions. Observation of life on this level should always be used to identify, assess, next strategize and then make things better.

- **Dormancy:** Dormancy is not safe in this area by any means, so try to avoid days and moments without some type of observation of yourself, your life and your surroundings. We lose track of ourselves and then unfortunately some lose their minds by not using this seed properly. Being unaware of constant life observation is a deadly game to play.

- **Germination:** Support its growth by evaluating your pursuits, your decisions, your surroundings, your associations, your accomplishments and the state of your heart, mind and spirit. Do this at least four times a year to maintain a greater connection with self. This helps you live more alert and better prepares you to deal with the future.

Chisinau

Moldova

"There is Greatness in everyone. It is the divine conscious light that gives us the power and desire to grow from the soil of existence and try to manifest a part of its greatness on the body of its eternal light through what we do and what we think we are."

-Denis Jurminschi

Ideologist | Writer | Software Developer | Entrepreneur

Atlanta, Georgia
United States of America

"Greatness is when you can be your authentic self in all relationships. Then you will live a rich, rewarding, and fulfilled life."

-Ken & Myra McKnight

President and CEO at A Better One is a Better Two

London, England
United Kingdom

"Greatness is the ability to continue despite setbacks and obstacles; to make a graceful comeback when you have been knocked down. To recognize that everyone is unique and blessed in their own way, to see the light in yourself, to uplift yourself whilst remaining humble and true. Working on yourself, learning, sharing, teaching, excelling and allowing the continuation of your personal growth without being hurtful to others, this is greatness."

-Danelle Harvey

Singer/Songwriter/Composer

Tygahoney Music & Publishing

BE GREAT.

It must become your mandated daily regimen to motivate yourself.

Stamford, Connecticut
United States of America

"Greatness to me is the ability to keep going when all seems impossible. It is consistently challenging yourself by overcoming fear to discover the unknown."

-Myrlande E. Sauveur

Author "Daily Spiritual Vitamins and Minerals for Your Soul"

Yeravan

Armenia

"Greatness means to me volition to forgiveness, this ability makes us like God. Greatness is vigilance of mind, physical activity of body and delicacy of soul. When I see an herb that grows cutting through the asphalt, it seems to me I see the Greatness."

-Narine Ananikyan

Singer & Soloist of National Opera and Ballet Theatre of Armenia

Portland, Oregon
United States of America

"I'm motivated by making an impact and creating a legacy. Of course those of us that tend to create a big wake can damage the waterfront, so we must be thoughtful. My approach to achieving greatness has been by giving more than I take. I've created and supported non-profits in my profession and community, both of which enable my success. Greatness is giving back and the more you give the more you get."

-Kent Lewis

President & Founder of Anvil & Formic Media

Gaborone
Botswana

"Greatness is being able to rise against all odds to make impact and leave the world better than you found it. It is being able to selflessly change lives of other people and in the process gain success. Greatness is creating a platform of excellence such that three or more generations to come, people will still celebrate your contributions to humanity."

-Wilbert R. Mutoko

Financial & Leadership Expert | Author | Speaker

Seed 19

SPEAK WITH A RUBY TONGUE

SPEAK WITH A RUBY TONGUE

Be careful of what you say dear friend. Do you not know that the power of life, death, success, poverty, depression, bondage, lack, happiness, freedom, weakness and strength are in your tongue? Our words are more valuable than money. They can cut faster than a switch blade or rescue a lonely soul on the verge of suicide. Speak with words that give life. Share sentences and conversations that uplift mankind, causing inspiration to spring up out of all that hear. Market hope and advertise endurance. Our society is quick to point out and promote the problems of the world for all to see. You must counter the negativity, not letting your outer language, which is symbolic of what is within you, bow down to the depressing mindsets of those around you. Speak With A Ruby Tongue, allowing value and optimism to be priority in what you say. Your words alone can change someone's life, even the entire world.

- **Seed Description:** Speak with purpose and positivity.

- **Soil:** Plant this into your daily conversations, especially those that lean toward negativity, doubt, and lack of faith.

- **Water:** Look for the good in all things and in all people, even if you believe there are none. There is a reason and purpose for everything. Sometimes bad things happen only for us to be able to share our experience and comfort with someone else who may endure the same thing. Even when you come across negative people, use that moment, internally, to appreciate how fortunate you are to think differently.

- **Oxygen:** Breathe life into this seed by constantly filling your life with the fruit from the same seed. Study the lives of those who embody this seed, who have produced fruit from it time and time again. Surround yourself with positivity in all things, no matter what or who it is. Consider this an atmosphere of greatness. You should constantly enter it or stay in it as much as possible for refueling and empowerment.

- **Temperature:** This seed is definitely one of the most powerful as you plant all your seeds of greatness. It carries inspiration and transfers life to everything it encounters. It is at the same time very exhilarating to grow this seed and also very dangerous if the growth process is not met with integrity, humility and a teachable spirit.

- **Light/Darkness:** The benefits of this seed far outweigh the disadvantages however not everyone likes "positive speaking people" these days. You'll have to know when to turn it up and when to lower the flame. Yes, this seed is a fire starter, it can change nations as well as cause others to stone you, desiring your death, as demonstrated several times in the past. Awareness is the key to balancing the use of this seed. Always remain ready though. People living in their greatness use this seed more in life than any other.

- **Dormancy:** I'm not perfect. You're not perfect. We're not perfect. Though I wish I could be everything to everyone, all positive, all energetic, all the time, I can't. With this particular seed, it's important to know that you are constantly giving out, perpetually releasing power from within you. If not careful and if you aren't taking in the same power from someone else or another source, you can exhaust yourself. This seeds thrives with the balance of releasing and receiving the same.

- **Germination:** Support its growth by thinking before you speak, by listening carefully to others first, so that you can precisely calculate and prepare strategic words to comfort or motivate in a certain situation. Be observant. The more you study people, the more information and details you will have in order to influence their decisions as well as know their next move.

Toronto, Ontario
Canada

"Greatness can be recognition but to me it is a statement of belief, that I've let go of fear to reach for my ideal, to stop playing it safe, see a reality and bring it to fruition."

-Eric Floresca

Freelance Writer

5:05pm - Time to be Great.

New York, New York
United States of America

"Greatness is inner peace. It is when you realize that you have the ability to make a difference. It is when you stop trying to live up to the standards of others, and when you can push forward alone, if need be."

-Stephanie Lynn Wilson

Actor | Writer | Director | Producer

Israel

"Greatness is doing good that significantly and positively impacts others. Greatness is the doctor who saves a life; the teacher who educates with true passion for preparing children's futures; the parent who raises children with unconditional love. Greatness is the dog whose persistent loyalty makes people strive to be better themselves. Greatness, like a fingerprint, is a quality we all possess uniquely, and it is up to each and every one of us to personify it to the best of our ability."

-Yasha Harari

Artist | Strategic Influencer

Austin, Texas
United States of America

"Greatness is losing with a smile and winning with tears in your eyes. It is also to always keep your integrity."

-Jaime L Furtado

Entrepreneur

BE BOLD.

Life only becomes life when you decide to live for it
and not just live because of it.

5:49pm - Time to be Great.

Yenagoa
Nigeria

"Knowing oneself and living ones purpose which transcends to making the world a better place for someone else to inhabit, that to me is Greatness."

-Barnabas McClint-Owei Ebiede

President MultiKoncepts LLC

Chicago, Illinois

United States of America

"Extracting insight from ones own crucibles and building the courage to own up to them is inspirational. Grasping the methods of mastery and acting upon them, makes one a success. Inspiring the multitude to challenge themselves to go through uncertain terrain, all in the effort to be better and do better is greatness."

-Seneca Brookins

Founder and CEO Jasudo Corp.

Copenhagen

Denmark

"Greatness is the day you discover that all the tools you can buy for money: Schools, Courses, Personal consulting Etc, Etc.. can help and guide you, but it will never make you successful. For being successful you need to have only 2 tools: Yourself and your will to always cross the "finish line" as number one."

-Anders Thorup

CEO & Co-Founder Global Oil Security

San Diego, California
United States of America

"Greatness comes by understanding the nobility of quiet. Quiet isn't shy; we need to release the negativity of that word and embrace its potential. Quiet is thoughtfully listening, sometimes followed by profound response, sometimes by reflection. Those wise enough to embrace quiet are working their path to self-realization and are innately aware that often silence, followed by thoughtful action, sometimes much later, helps us grow to become gloriously great human beings."

-Lynda Dearborn Pietroforte

Nursing and System Recruiter at Sharp HealthCare

Seed 20
AS THE WATER FLOWS

AS THE WATER FLOWS

Even when water is still, it continues to provide movement and life. So why would you stop or give up? We should be like water, always flowing or giving life to something or someone. It doesn't matter where you've been or what you've been through, you still have life, movement is present, so you must continue. Water washes away, it strengthens, it quenches by providing a solution, it heals, and it transfers things from place to place. We have the mission of living as the water flows. Washing away old thought processes that have held our families and communities in captivity. Strengthening our friends and peers who need encouragement. Quenching the hunger for wisdom and knowledge in others by sharing what we know. Healing the fainted hearts of millions by letting them know we care. Transferring dreams to reality by opening doors for others to succeed. You shall live as the water flows, and even when your journey ends, that water will continue to flow forever, from person to person, over and over again.

- **Seed Description:** Let your life be a multi-purpose change agent, like water

- **Soil:** Plant this into moments where change and new thought processes are mandatory. Many people suffer because no one was ever honest enough to tell them what they need to do to become greater.

- **Water:** Water this seed with a philanthropic heart, one that lives to make things better for all.

- **Oxygen:** Breathe life into this seed by gathering others to flow as water. Most people really do want to make a difference yet they wait to see someone else do it first. Be that someone, let it flow.

- **Temperature:** We live in perilous times. Anything can happen at any moment, therefore we must work while we can to make the best from what we have before us. Tomorrow is never promised. Let your greatness come forth now to better every person and situation you encounter.

- **Light/Darkness:** Change is risky. Change is dangerous. Change is controversial. Change is also inevitable. World changers don't care about the status quo, neither do they pay attention to those who care about it. No matter the praise or blame you receive, be led by your heart and your passion, never let the water cease flowing.

- **Dormancy:** There are seasons when change must be silent and wait. During these moments we should prepare for a greater return, a mightier rush, your most powerful flow. Greatness should always increase.

- **Germination:** Support its growth by being authentic in everything you do and say. Do things for others because you truly have a desire to. Flow like water to the world because it comes natural to you. Authenticity and integrity in your words and actions in public and behind closed doors is greatness at its best.

Kampala
Uganda

"Greatness is being able to point others away from your own mistakes and to their success by lessons of your own life."

-Godfrey Epodoi

General Manager Divine Shuttles

Minneapolis, Minnesota
United States of America

"No matter what people do, when they do it from their heart they do it best and shine brightest. I've been blessed to be surrounded by great people in my life: My daddy whose heart was in his faith and family; my sister Terri, a nurse practitioner whose heart is in caring for others; my partner Mike, whose heart is in the joy of authentic relationships; I have been touched by many hearts modeling Greatness for me."

-Lori Ruff

CEO Integrated Alliances

Lisbon
Portugal

"Greatness is helping someone become greater than yourself and when that specific person turns back to you and say that you are the one responsible for their success. Being generous is definitely being great."

-Pedro Malheiro

CEO Edge Innovation

BE WISE.

Opportunities are endless, they have no measure and they are active every waking moment of your life if you focus on them.

Denver, Colorado

United States of America

"Greatness in my mind is trusting, believing in yourself with unwavering focus and definiteness of purpose to accomplishing your dreams despite adversity. After manifestation of ones dreams, being still in love with self and sharing that love with all others."

-Robin J

Owner/Djiva Principle Productions

Creator/Cirque De Femme II Women Empowerment Series

Trinidad and Tobago

"Greatness is living a positive and productive life with passion, gratitude and generosity. Greatness is achieved by living in line with your values and expressing your unique gifts and talents all while in harmony with others."

-Leah de Souza

Training and Development Consultant

San Diego, California
United States of America

"Greatness is expressing all your own unique creative potential and inspiring everyone you touch to fulfill theirs, in spite of fear, doubt or naysayers. Almost everyone we think of as great artists, innovators or entrepreneurs had to surmount all these. In hindsight, their success seems inevitable...but while we celebrate their creativity or vision, we often forget the courage it took to persevere at a time when voices around them --perhaps including their own -- told them they were wasting their time, and should "get a real job."

-Lisa Rothstein

Marketing Consultant | Copywriter | Cartoonist

Algiers
Algeria

"Greatness is to be master of oneself."

-Faris Bouchaala

CEO Agence Premiere

Seed 21
INTERNAL

INTERNAL

$\mathscr{I}$have learned throughout my years on Earth that the must

powerful place in the world resides inside of you. What goes on inside an individual determines the outcome of what they release into the world and into the lives of others. You have influence in what happens, what can happen and what you won't allow to happen. It all starts within, paying attention to that inner voice, taking time to listen to yourself, blocking out all the voices of friends, family, co-workers, and popular media. The most successful and globally influential people in the world have mastered the internal. It inspires you, it motivates you, it's there to guide you, if you just seek to know that which is within. The best way to know who you are is to discover the origin from which you were created. I know there is a God and He alone created your internal atmosphere. So start there and just ask. You have nothing to lose. As you grow, your ideas, your decisions, and your pursuits should originate from your internal self. This my friend represents the beginning of fulfilling your life purpose and multiple destinations.

- **Seed Description:** Live internally to soar externally.

- **Soil:** Plant this seed into decisions that involve what you want to achieve and where you want to go in life.

- **Water:** Water this by meditation. It is only when we are truly alone that we are able to engulf and embrace the magnitude our entire inner being, to hear and to listen to self and to spirit.

- **Oxygen:** Breathe life into this seed by trusting your gut instinct when you come across situations where you have to make a quick decision or decide something on behalf of a group or individual. Greatness will automatically place you before people and in decision making positions, so it is imperative your internal instinct operates on an advanced level when it comes to this.

- **Temperature:** The more you rely on that which is within to guide you, the more you'll realize how many people around you are not doing the same. Don't let this frustrate you, instead use your enlightenment and awareness strategically to pull one person at a time into this new realm of living.

- **Light/Darkness:** It's not popular to seek internal direction on everything. Most people have become so busy, consumed, distracted and occupied until they forget to check-in with their heart, even on some of the biggest decisions they are faced with. No matter what and no matter how short of a time frame you have, to save you future heartache and wasted time, I advise you to always step to the side and communicate with self. There's nothing so important in this lifetime that you should rush to do unless you are guided by a higher power to do so. One thought-out right decision can take you to the top of the mountain. One rushed wrong decision can place you below the surface.

- **Dormancy:** There are moments when it's hard to decipher what exactly is being said within. There are occasional conflicts, especially when options have benefits on both sides. In times of dormancy where you feel complacent or blocked, just wait. Wait and sleep on it. It may take a little more time for everything to fully filtrate into your mind, heart and spirit in order for you to make the next move. Some things in life have to be sifted so you can see what you're really getting out of the deal. Wait it out, see what happens over the next few days or in some cases, weeks. In situations like these, waiting is next to genius.

- **Germination:** Support its growth by listening to yourself, paying attention to the inner voices and promptings that we all have. There is a purpose and a reason for them. Don't ignore the person within, your inner man is there to walk beside you and soar with you. Love the person you are, inside and out. When no one else is around, you will have to rely on your internal self and inner strength to get through tough moments.

Zurich
Switzerland

"Greatness is building an entrepreneurship foundation for the super poor villagers in our imperfect world of human failures for over 300 years."

-James C.A. Tay

Business Development Partner Aceh Invest

Florida
United States of America

"Greatness is the ability to push yourself to your limits and go beyond them to achieve the goals you have set for your self. It is having the inner strength to not have any excuses not to succeed, having the power to enlighten the people around you, to be empowered, endearing, compassionate, and thankful to those who help you to achieve what others may think is impossible. Greatness is Me, for we are all great in our own way."

-Jermaine Lewis

Diary Editor at Nielsen

Micronesia

"Greatness is standing your ground in what you believe in and doing what is just for humanity. Fear is that lack of faith in yourself."

-Jonathan Mathau

Mathau Anglers and Y.E.S.

Atlanta, Georgia
United States of America

"Greatness to me is the ability to harness ones skills, talents, and ability and apply an unsurpassed work ethic and willingness to win, with the understanding that failure is not a destination, but a part of the process."

-James B. Kynes, Jr.

CEO The Ultimate Lifestyle Grooming Brands

BE GREAT.

Change is risky. Change is dangerous. Change is controversial. Change is also inevitable.

British Columbia

Canada

"Greatness is the ability to master the small details that make the most difference."

-Ruben Dias

Serial Entrepreneur | Smart Money Investor

Houston, Texas

United States of America

"Greatness is not being egotistical, diplomatically facilitating others without envisaging reimbursement. Anticipating the best in others and under no circumstances criticize them. Instead disclose your testimony to inspire and foster others to excel by divine exemplar. When others comprehend what you have be subjected to; on the way to acquiring what was destined for you that exposes greatness. Transpiring into a manipulating motivator exudes greatness."

-Angela Banks-Pete

Recruitment Marketing Manager

Panama

"There is a Great One from where all greatness comes, our job is not to be great but to imitate His greatness and the closer we get to doing this in our lives, the closer we will get to that greatness we so much seek. It has all been done for us to follow, there is nothing new for us to invent."

-Gustavo A. Troncoso

CEO PGS Corporate Multinational Group

Seed 22
DOMINION

DOMINION

When you know your God, He knows who you are, then He tells the world. Oh how I long for the day when mankind wakes up and realizes our divine inheritance. We are more than just people, more than citizens, more than black, white, Asian, Hispanic, etc. We are a unique creation, geniuses indeed, placed on Earth to rule it and maintain it for the betterment of all people. Oh how ashamed we should be, raising our kids as regular people. Oh how sad we have become, letting material things and personalities define our importance and value. Our minds can create almost anything, and everyday a new invention or innovation springs forth. Every disease on Earth has its cure also on Earth. Nothing can enter this sacred realm without first the solution. You were born to dominate, lead, change, inspire, heal and infiltrate the world. Who on this Earth can deny the power that is within you? No one because it is given individually. Take the limits off who you think you are and who you appear to be to others. Dominion. Control over your perception of you produces boldness to obtain influence over whatever you desire. Dominion. Understanding that you are you, doing something everyday to make yourself wiser and better, increases your dominion reach.

- **Seed Description:** Take authority over your life, what comes in and what goes out, what you need to learn, what you need to teach, what you produce and contribute to the world, and what you give to others to follow.

- **Soil:** Plant this into every moment you have alive, otherwise your life will be passive and leave little for others to emulate.

- **Water:** Decide that you want to be more, to be better, to desire the best in everything and to remain curious and hungry for knowledge. The idea of dominion is not just to dominate, but also to soar and be well informed on a variety of things so that you can intervene or be of use in many different situations and environments. Limits rarely accompany greatness.

- **Oxygen:** Some things in life we can't change but most of them we can. This is greatness, knowing that the power to change most things is not only in you but also up to you. Use this power and knowledge towards your plans and goals, also towards helping others out in some way.

- **Temperature:** Most people never use the seed of dominion. They are rarely introduced to it within their circle. This is why it is important to expand your surroundings, network, and pursue more than what is expected. Greatness is always expanding, even when you've mastered certain things, greatness looks for something new.

- **Light/Darkness:** This is seed commonly associated with leaders, high-powered businessman and women, those that stand in front crowds, rule nations, and guide large groups of people but this seed should also be found in parents, students, community leaders, and everyday people. You don't have to run a billion dollar corporation but you do have to run your life as if it's worth the same or even more. This is the key to dominion, accessing your value and then living in every way possible to increase it while helping others do the same. You will face isolation with dominion. This seed doesn't have many siblings living nearby, but if you search, you will come across others in due time.

- **Dormancy:** Dominion should never go dormant. Your awareness of everything related to dominion should remain keen throughout life once you've been introduced to it.

- **Germination:** Support your own dominion, internally and externally, by demanding more from yourself, and then gradually from those around you as well. Don't expect everyone to follow right away but do make an effort to push others into a higher life when you can. Most people lack and suffer because of a lack of knowledge. If you don't show them, tell them and teach them, they will never know their potential.

London, England

United Kingdom

"Greatness is about achieving my life destiny and living a life through acquisition of inner peace, happiness, fulfillment, personal and financial freedom through the power of positive thinking, gift of intuition and wisdom while also connecting with like-minded positive people from diverse cultures. Greatness is also about utilizing the gift of wisdom to embrace a higher spiritual awareness, achieving a balanced mental, physical emotional and psychological well being. Greatness is discovering who I am and why I have been born into this world."

-Genevieve Flight

Author | Speaker | CEO | Personal Coach

Cleveland, Ohio
United States of America

"Recognizing that you cannot control what others say or do, that you can only control your reaction to those words and actions, has been the catalyst for my inner greatness to rise to the surface. One cannot reach their full potential if they are allowing themselves to be grounded by the words and actions of others, so unshackle yourself from negativity and achieve your greatness."

-ReGina Crawford

CEO G Styl Productions

San Pedro Sula

Honduras

*"Greatness is understand that there is nothing greater
or less..."*

-Cristian Molina

Director | Actor | Producer

New York, New York

United States of America

"Greatness is the feeling of being free to create the best."

-Anastasia Gamezo

PR Manager

BE BOLD.

Every day is an open door to walk into the extraordinary, it's all a matter of perception, ideas, focus and strategy.

Namibia

"Greatness for me entails living a life where you set goals and then you back them up with commitment as well as passion to successfully see them to fruition. It is all about having the integrity first to yourself and thereafter to others, to work as much as you can to make those goals a reality."

-Frans Mupura

National Development Advisor at Office of the President
National Planning Commission

Sacramento, California

United States of America

"Greatness is learning the rules and then throwing them out the window. Stay true to who you are despite what is expected and acceptable. Never be afraid to be and do what works for you."

-A. Michelle Blakeley

Managing Partner Solar Hygienics, LLC

Ferizaj

Kosovo

"Greatness is what makes you feel like superhero. It feels everything you touch, you make it work. By that, all you need in your life is to be Great at what you do."

-Flakerim Ismani

Founder Urbanway LLC

Chicago, Illinois
United States of America

"Greatness is being able to have the ability, knowledge and common sense to separate those things in life that are good or bad. In order to achieve greatness you must remove all negative things that stand in the way of you achieving your goals."

-Joyce Parker

CEO Wonder Marketing & Referral Service

Seed 23
AN HONOR

AN HONOR

To know who you are is an advantage to yourself. To know your Creator is an advantage to the world. There are several things an individual will never realize and never experience until they have a real relationship with God. Whether you believe in Him or not, I, myself, have found this to be true. Everything ever created has a purpose. Look at the inventions around you, they all have a purpose or they wouldn't be needed. I believe your ultimate purpose is directly tied to knowing God, who He is, what He is about, and why He allowed you to be here. It then becomes an honor to start a friendship and relationship with the infinite and all-powerful. Let it be your prayer to open up to the one who is with you and forever within you. You are loved beyond measure. Trust me on this. It takes one second to believe and a lifetime to not believe.

- **Seed Definition:** A relationship with God.

- **Soil:** Plant this into your daily life. Get to know your Creator.

- **Water:** Water this seed by spending time observing God's awesome creations as far as the animals, nature, fruits, vegetables, grains, rain, sunlight and more, all these amazing things that were created as provision for us, which never ends.

- **Oxygen:** Meditate and research to learn more about those in the past who sought after and relied on God. Some of the greatest businessmen and women of our time have proclaimed the blessings of prayer.

- **Temperature:** God may be beyond our full comprehension but as His creation, His spirit is a part of us. Knowing this, we don't have to go anywhere to find Him. It's all a matter of looking within and starting a conversation.

- **Light/Darkness:** We all know the topic of God is a heated one, for some, so don't expect a standing ovation for your beliefs when it comes to this seed. Some will agree with you while others feel life can be much easier by not believing in anything. Well, to not believe is also a belief. I know what works for me and it is with this conviction that I share it with you. I remain in awe from what I have experienced, the people I've met and now of course, the global magnitude of this writing, joined by hundreds of friends around the world, since asking God to lead my journey of life years ago.

- **Dormancy:** Believe it or not, there can be dormancy periods in your walk or relationship with God. As humans we get distracted, we get caught up in people and things, placing God to the side at our own convenience, until we're ready to progress with Him again. And many times, He allows it. Then after everything comes crashing down on us, we run back to Him and He's there waiting, graciously waiting, because His commitment to us is forever.

- **Germination:** Support its growth by surrounding yourself with like-minded believers, those who will encourage your relationship and enhance it. Also ask God more questions, feel free to communicate your thoughts, He already knows them so you might as well talk about it. God is much closer than what we've been taught. Once you truly realize this and tap into the closeness, which is followed by the power and the creative spirit, the world will open to you and allow you to add whatever you desire to this place called Earth.

Indonesia

"Greatness is the ability to keep on reinventing yourself until you get to the fullest best version of you."

-Sartika Kurniali

Author | Faculty Member and Evernote Writing Ambassador

Las Vegas, Nevada

United States of America

"Greatness is knowing that your life means something to more people than you know personally."

-Michael Franklin

Administrator MCNM Marketing Network

Toronto, Ontario
Canada

"Greatness is the will to fight against seemingly insurmountable obstacles and outwit fate, betting against the most unbelievable odds and winning. Greatness lies in neither being drunk on success or browbeaten by misfortune. Greatness depends on defending the beautiful, the true, and the good while sailing through a world of grey. Greatness means singing out for Life and Light. Greatness is found in rising again, from nothing, after you are thought vanquished by all."

-Charles Boissoneau-Nunno

Actor | Writer at We Make Movies

BE WISE.

The more aware you are of your inner genius, which is also God, the more you will produce.

Nashville, Tennessee
United States of America

"Greatness is showing humility, dignity and respect to others while pursuing ways to improve our world."

-Lynda F. Jones

Managing Member at The Jones Law Group PLLC

Germany

"Greatness is the ability to stand up every time you fall down and to notice the opportunity behind."

-Markus C. Mueller

Former CEO of Ubitexx (acquired by BlackBerry)

Sarasota, Florida

United States of America

"Greatness, being perceived as level of strength and prestige, is to me a measure of one's ability to complete a task in which he/she has been assigned. With life being the most immense assignment, one must be able to realize the potential in their lives and professional careers while at the same time subjugate the dilemmas that may impede progress."

-Matthew Lasker

Account Executive at RCT Disaster Recovery

Kg Sireh Naka Kedah

Malaysia

"Greatness is being humble within yourself, with others and mother nature as a whole. The universe speaks to us everyday, we just need to feel and hear the senses of the inner and outer of our soul. The path of your journey is linked to many doors that the universe wants to embrace with kindness and solitude."

-Zulkifly Haji Jamaudin

Owner Z-J'S

Seed 24

A BROKEN HEART

A BROKEN HEART

It hurts, like a deep wound that never gets any medical attention. It bleeds, like a river with no ending. It cries, day & night, only taking short breaks like a newborn baby. When your heart is broken it feels like living has no meaning. You want the world to stop and help, so that you don't feel alone. I've often wondered, what is the purpose of the broken heart? To learn a lesson, to produce a desire to help someone? Or maybe it's to prove the point that all things can heal with time? Could it be so that it helps us to not be the cause of future broken hearts? I say yes to all. Experiencing a broken heart in any way is not meant to shut you down, but instead, it's to help you help yourself, and ultimately someone else. Let the pain you feel become the future knowledge for another person. Take the pain you experience in life and use it to change the world for the better.

- **Seed Description:** Redirecting pain towards greatness.

- **Soil:** Plant this into your toughest emotional moments in life, when the pain feels insurmountable and at its greatest.

- **Water:** Water this seed by understanding that pain is a part of life. We all experience at some point and we can't run from it. This we must face as human beings yet still, eventually rebound. We must accept that we were built to withstand all kinds of turmoil and sadness. We are overcomers by heart and resilient by spirit.

- **Oxygen:** It's very wise to be connected with those who know more than you and those who have experienced things that you haven't. Some people prefer to learn the hard way and on their own but why place yourself in harms way when you can learn from someone else's mistakes. Learn what you can from those who have already walked the path. Don't make your life any harder or more complicated than life already is.

- **Temperature:** Pain can be very dangerous. It is suggestive, persuasive, convincing and often misleading. If we aren't aware of the type of pain we encounter, it can cause us to make irrational decisions and respond in a way that questions our integrity while aiming to tarnish our dignity. Upon arrival of emotional pain, analyze the situation, don't make any quick decisions. Pray, wait, pray again. Your greatness will always be tested through pain or power.

- **Light/Darkness:** Life is an experience and a journey, which means that every part of life can teach us something. This is the best way to grow and remain in a progressive state of mind throughout life, no matter what comes your way. We open ourselves up for failure, depression, hatred, ignorance and death when we allow an unteachable spirit to live and breathe within us.

- **Dormancy:** There are times of pain when all you can do is cry. I've been there several times. The tears must come out, they will eventually so go ahead and let them roll. They only reflect that you have a heart, so don't be ashamed of

323

that. Pain can cripple you temporarily and momentarily but it doesn't have the power, the authority, or know-how to stop you. I believe time heals all yet it's our responsibility to encourage ourselves, day in and day out, to make the healing process faster.

- **Germination:** Learn from pain. When we learn from our mistakes we grow. When we don't learn from our mistakes that cause pain, we slowly die inside, emotionally then physically, damaging and weakening the heart more and more until it finally decides to give up. Use pain to grow and to become greater, this is the only reason it stops by your life.

Helsingborg

Sweden

"Greatness is the courage to live an honest life towards yourself and others. True honesty is facing and facilitating all your strengths and weaknesses into one glorious self image full of acceptance and love. When you start being honest about yourself, the world starts being true. Honesty creates true vision, and a true vision combined with execution can change the world."

-Daniel Nüüd

Founder/Lead Coach Hybris Empire

Chicago, Illinois
United States of America

"Greatness is pushing past limiting beliefs to distinguish your purpose in life and in doing so transforming your life and the lives of others. It is the ability to walk in the face of adversity, and ignore the still small voice in your head that challenges you so can achieve and be all that you were born to be."

-Melissa Krivachek

President of Briella Arion

Iran

"To be helpful to others. Not to be put off by obstacles on your way to achieve what you strive for. To Radiate Love in your actions and deeds. Think of new ideas and have perseverance in implementing them. Go after what you love."

-Bahram Razavi-Malaki

Founder and Mgr. Long Span Bridges Subcommittee at Iranian Society of Consulting Engineers

Mesa, Arizona
United States of America

"Greatness is accomplishing something you set out to do to the best of your ability, to do so with no regrets as to the outcome. One can set out to achieve many different goals in any time and point in life and be happy that you got an earnest chance to try. It can also be enabling and/or helping someone else achieve their goals and be sincerely happy for them even if they did better than you. If you do achieve something 'world class' then you use that notoriety as a role model for others. However, greatness does not necessarily mean that you become well known but that in the end you have many people attend your funeral but not enough time for all that want to give you a eulogy."

-Jeff Hodgkinson

Program Manager

BE GREAT.

You are responsible for releasing your own greatness in your lifetime.

Mandaluyong
Philippines

"Greatness is far beyond expectations, immortal, and non-transferable."

-Paulo Santos

SEO Expert

Atlanta, Georgia
United States of America

"To me, greatness is best associated with the virtue of service. It is exciting to know that Germaine Moody's book launch of "50 Seeds of Greatness" coincides with the exact 50th Anniversary of Dr. King's world-famous speech "I Have A Dream!"

-John R. Naugle

CEO of Atlanta: City of Peace, Inc. (ACP)

Montevideo

Uruguay

"For me, Greatness is planting good and fertile seeds without the expectation to receive anything in return."

-Javier Zerbino

Founder Zmartmedia

Seed 25
CHARGE UP

CHARGE UP

This is it. This is your one chance to make something

spectacular of your life. What you do today really does determine what will happen in the future. So get up! Encourage yourself, become a best friend to yourself, open your mind to new things, surround yourself with people that motivate you. In order to experience your own continual greatness, you must learn to recharge your inner person, your spirit. Life can be exhausting, the uncertainties, the responsibilities, the everyday cares that consume us, leaving us tired, weary, and for some, depressed. When things get too overwhelming, take a moment, pray, calm down, pause. Rest and refresh yourself. This moment of frustration won't last forever. You are not a quitter and you're not a loser. Maintain inner reserves of Courage and Motivation, which gives you endless power. You will need these throughout life, not just for yourself, but to share with others in their time of need.

- **Seed Description:** Stay invigorated.

- **Soil:** Plant this into moments when all you want to do is give up and throw in the towel.

- **Water:** Water this seed by receiving the power of self-encouragement. Even when no one else around has a positive outlook, it becomes your duty to be that person.

- **Oxygen:** Encourage others when they need motivation. Lend a helping hand or a word of inspiration. Little do we know how much God stores up for our own time of need by what we do for others.

- **Temperature:** You have to wake up with expectation. Never let people or society dictate how your day will be. We awake to all kinds of problems going on around the world and many times in our lives, but problems come with life, so don't let them throw you off balance. Arise knowing that you have the power to make the day what it shall be and that your presence will enhance someone else's day as well.

- **Light/Darkness:** What you project outwardly to the world in person must become more than just a positive attitude because attitudes change with the wind and season. Become what you believe, live it daily in actions and words, making and claiming everyday as a great day, no matter what happens. This is the evidence of greatness, to become what wasn't, what is, and to remain, never uprooted during the earthquakes of life.

- **Dormancy:** Let your dormancy moments be few and short. What you carry within cannot be silenced for long because so many people need to be enlightened as several suffer from lack of hope.

- **Germination:** Stay charged up and invigorated by the company you keep and by the words they preach. Make sure your core circle of friends and colleagues are a group of productive and progressive individuals. If everyone around you is sad, upset, angry, and feeling defeated, then now is the time to meet new people, network, and find those focused on living in their greatness as well.

Dhaka

Bangladesh

*"Greatness, to me, is about positively impacting people's
lives. The more people impacted, the greater the greatness."*

-Tarek Kamal

CEO iNFiNiTi HR Company Limited

Denver, Colorado
United States of America

"Greatness is knowing what it is to be content in matters of life, while loving and engaging fully, regardless of the outcome."

-Ashley E. Kingsley

CMO at Red Thread Creative Group

Vietnam

"Greatness is continuous and tireless problem solving. A never-give-up attitude with superior leadership."

-Csaba Bundik

Board Member ALTERA Wealth Management

BE BOLD.

To truly become great, you must proactively challenge yourself, even more so than the natural obstacles that will come against you in life.

Austin, Texas

United States of America

"Greatness is when you confront your deepest fears by taking action that contradicts those fears."

-Elise Krentzel

Founder at LifeGPS | Transformation Coach

London, England
United Kingdom

"Greatness is the caring, strong and intelligent thing inside all of us that encourages us to push ourselves and others to be the best that we can be."

-Holly Dover

Receptionist

Riverside, California

United States of America

"Greatness is knowing your passion, purpose and your worth in life, and going after it with full force. You may fall a few times, but that just makes you stronger so that once you reach a certain point you will be able to mentor others on how to get there. Greatness is learning, applying and teaching."

-Naomi Bonman

Journalist | Publicist | Screen Writer

Mauritius

"True greatness is achieved when people still remember you for great things you have done even after you die."

-Sumaroo Suyash Kumar

Founder Calopi

Seed 26
SUCCESS

SUCCESS

Success is an internal atmosphere. The external will manifest itself naturally. Though the world may look at success as having lots of money, influence, power, great achievements and so on, I believe true success begins with you loving and accepting yourself for who you are. Success starts right there. This can't be taken away and no other person can be more successful at that than you. Once this is established, any outside success is only to be used to lead and inspire others. True success will always make someone else a success along the way. So ask yourself, who am I making a success? Until you can answer that question, you haven't really experienced success, you've only been experiencing accomplishments, which none of them go with you when you leave this life. Success should always breed more success, which produces your legacy.

- **Seed Description:** Success on the inside, success on the outside, success forever.

- **Soil:** Plant this seed into your mind, let it replace what the outside world has taught you about how to measure success.

- **Water:** Water this seed by getting to know yourself, your talents, skills, wants, desires, what makes you sad, what makes you happy, the things you want to change about the world and so on. This helps you establish who you are, which makes it easier to find life direction.

- **Oxygen:** Study the life of those who embody not only success on the outside but those who you believe carry integrity and humility in the midst of their influence or monetary gain, those that continue to use and share their success with others also.

- **Temperature:** There are different types of success and different definitions of it per person. Some consider being successful is to simply be happy in life. Others believe it means to be well-off financially with a great family and great friends. Definitions vary, they will always differ however no success is ever complete unless another success can be birthed from it in some way.

- **Light/Darkness:** Career success can be the best thing that ever happens in your life. It can give you notoriety, influence, power, access, and it can also generate great wealth. Success can be the exact opposite if you don't take the time to investigate the potential downsides of it. With any type of real success, there will be sacrifice. It can be time, money, friends, family, lovers, or anything that stands in the way of it. Approach success with wisdom and balance. Wisdom to help you discern that which is authentic and those around you who are genuine. Balance to help you properly measure the cost against the reward, so that you come out lacking nothing, without regret, yet instead with gratitude and the right spirit to share your experience and your new insight.

- **Dormancy:** There are times when it looks like no success is in view. It's easy to grow weary during the process of becoming successful in a particular goal or pursuit. Understand that the success is in the pursuit, you've already surpassed millions who didn't even have the courage to begin. Success always starts within. Nothing would ever begin without something inside of you mentioning it or agreeing first.

- **Germination:** Support its growth by remaining curious and focused, asking questions, connecting with those who know things that you don't, researching, creating moments of solitude to check-in with yourself periodically, and observing the characteristics of successful individuals in the past and present.

Dubai

United Arab Emirates

"Greatness starts from the very basics of understanding your inner self and the cause of being a human being. The day one understands this basic phenomena, all knots of life get opened. Deep down, you can understand the meaning of yourself, your existence, and your being for the world. Only then you can lend yourself, your spirits and your emotions to someone in great way(s). A billionaire helping poor with peanuts or a poor person helping others with all his/her wealth creates a big difference of greatness. Greatness is thinking beyond yourself."

-Farah Shahbano

Mother | Banker

8:15am - Time to be Great.

Bloomington, Indiana
United States of America

"Greatness is...that special knowing or inner resolve one has, knowing that they were meant to serve selflessly some higher purpose in serving humanity in fulfilling their life mission."

-Liz Isaacs

Author | Personal Development Life Coach Lotus Motivations

Barbados

"Having as much faith or potential as a mustard seed, and the influence on its surroundings demonstrates true greatness."

-Ryan Boyce

Founder of Caribbean Musician & The 100 Voice Project

Chicago, Illinois
United States of America

"Greatness is when you see past all the noise, the negative, and the naysayers. When you give it your all knowing you've done your best to give back the talents God gave you. That's what He expects, - to use your abilities and talents every moment of every day. When you give your best to others, and expect nothing in return, then you have achieved greatness."

-Bryce, Johnathon, and Clayton Mann

REBELMANN Rock Band

BE WISE.

The most powerful forces on Earth are unseen, they can only be expressed or demonstrated.

Durban

South Africa

"To me, true greatness is the soulmate of humility. A great person is one who - no matter how rich, successful or powerful they may be - will still afford another person, no matter what their standing in life, give them the respect and dignity that they deserve as a fellow human being."

-Barry Tuck

The Guy Who Does Stuff Paton Tupper Digital

Atlanta, Georgia

United States of America

"Greatness is realizing your destiny and accepting the responsibility. Greatness is overcoming fears and challenges in order to fulfill that destiny. Greatness is achieving, even in the presence of your "Judas". Greatness is sacrificing in order to better future generations. Greatness is eternal!"

-JAY B.A.D.A.

Entertainment Professional

Cameroon

"Greatness is the willingness to find solutions to problems that will help enhance lifestyle and habits with the ability of fairness and the desire to share!"

-Julius Dohnji

Director Bumalla Investment Ventures

Seed 27
FAVOR

FAVOR

It is finished. There is an atmosphere where everything doesn't work out as planned but where everything works out for your good, and in your best long-term interest. It's an atmosphere of expectancy and certainty. Favor is a realm of privilege and access set in place for release and mobility at any given moment. Many have asked how to obtain it? My reply, favor chooses you. It comes from the Creator and He makes the final decision. I do believe you can ask for it in prayer but if you do, beware. Favor doesn't come cheap. It comes with a responsibility, a mission, a purpose, something meaningful that changes lives. Never confuse 'luck' and 'favor'. Luck is temporary and seasonal while favor usually starts at birth and lasts a lifetime. Do not be ignorant of favor, it causes many to envy you. Stand your ground, remain focused, and use favor to complete your mission on Earth.

- **Seed Description:** Favor in life.

- **Soil:** Plant this into your entire life, observing constantly as things happen on your behalf that normally doesn't happen for others.

- **Water:** Water this seed with the spirit of gratitude, always remaining grateful no matter what.

- **Oxygen:** Use the favor that is poured in your life to be a blessing to others. You don't have to explain yourself, just share what you receive and what you know. A heart of thanks, appreciation and philanthropy perpetuates continual favor.

- **Temperature:** Not everyone gets to experience supernatural and unexplainable great things during their lifetime, so at some point, it will become obvious to you that there's something different going on concerning you. Favor opens the door for even more greatness to come in.

- **Light/Darkness:** It's sad that everyone won't be happy for your happiness. Add favor to your happiness and you'll create some very envious onlookers. No worries, it comes with the territory. Use your favor to enhance the lives of others, that way they won't have time to envy yours.

- **Dormancy:** If you're like me, you want to always feel like something amazing is happening or about to happen, but there are times when you'll feel like nothing is happening or even feel like favor is on vacation. When you have feelings of dormancy, look back on past moments of favor. This will help you remain confident. Favor is for a lifetime yet only appears when it's needed.

- **Germination:** Support its growth with gratitude, prayer and using your favor to serve others.

New York, New York

United States of America

"Greatness transforms seeds of growth to full-grown cherry blossom trees. It's in building and inspiring thought leaders through harmony, integrity, conscionable action and multiplicity."

-Caryn Chow

Caryn Chow International, Founder of Propel Your Dreams!™ and 7prettywomen

Argentina

"Greatness is sharing your wisdom and knowledge with the people, and enjoying their success more than your own."

-Gustavo Stecher

Co-Founder at imagenHB

Addison, Texas

United States of America

"Greatness takes on many forms: Parents, teachers, doctors, law enforcement officers, and firemen just to name a few. Helping others to be their best in life without thought of themselves is greatness."

-Brian Reid

Regional Sales Director | Accelerated Depreciation Specialists

BE GREAT.

When we don't create, we lose parts of our soul and we stagnate this divine characteristic.

Vancouver, British Columbia

Canada

"Greatness is knowing and loving yourself. It is continuously gaining insights into who you are, accepting your place on your life's path, continuously working to become your best self. It is not pleasing others, measuring against benchmarks or attaining praise. It is enjoying the journey."

-Chris Goward

Founder WiderFunnel Marketing Optimization

Author of "You Should Test That!" | Keynote Speaker

San Jose, California

United States of America

"Greatness is the ability to follow your passion with 100% of your heart. By not allowing anyone or anything to influence your pursuit of your passion, you will become so devoted to it that there is absolutely no way you will not achieve greatness."

-Ric Kostick

CEO 100% Pure

Benin

"For me, greatness is a value. Moreover, it is a virtue. Wise people behave with greatness. Well, it is the capacity of someone to be different through his or her good practices."

-Gambadatoun Georges

Entrepreneur | Translator

Denver, Colorado
United States of America

"What greatness means to me is making it as a black American, single or married male, in this life as a family man, citizen, professional, entrepreneur and God man. Achieving the vision that God has given you with the strength, courage, valiant, faith, health, leadership, and guidance to build and leave a legacy of prosperity, and hope for the future generation of his seed."

-Brian Beecher

President & CEO at Joules Technology Inc.

Seed 28
WONDERFUL PEOPLE

WONDERFUL PEOPLE

Just in case you haven't noticed by now, life isn't easy, well not for the majority, but there are people strategically placed throughout your lifetime to cheer you up, assist you, confirm what you're doing is right and to come to your rescue. These are the 'Wonderful People', those that operate in courage, joy, peace, philanthropy and motivation. The more you operate as one, the more of them you will meet. Throughout my travels I've met thousands. We live in a society where bad news always takes center stage. You won't hear much low-minded talking around these people though, they'd rather be discussing a solution or resolution to make something better. Do you believe in angels? I do. Are 'Wonderful People' angels? They could be, I believe some are. When we're operating at our best, we all can appear angelic. The Bible does say that angels are among us (Hebrews 13:2). Keep an eye, ear and your spirit open to recognize these people. I often refer to many as my "Destiny Team". Don't forget to look into the mirror today, that's where they all started.

- **Seed Description:** Your awareness of Wonderful People or your "Destiny Team". Those that appear when needed to make sure you continue and move forward.

- **Soil:** Plant the awareness of this seed into every encounter with another person. Discern whether or not they belong in your life for a reason or a season.

- **Water:** Water this by awareness, observation, alertness and evaluation of everything going on around you on a daily basis.

- **Oxygen:** You are also considered to be a part of this group by others. So breathe life into this seed by recognizing who considers you a part of their destiny team. When several people unite to all help each other, impossibilities are the last thing on their mind.

- **Temperature:** Some people are sent temporarily but they can still play a significant role in your progression and greatness. Some may be around for a lifetime. They all operate differently. Some may not appear as nice as others. Many are sent to push you not pamper you, so be aware and receptive to their aggression, it's only to make you greater.

- **Light/Darkness:** Many suffer because of a lack of knowledge, which I must repeat. They aren't aware of this information when it comes to people they meet or the kind of people they should be seeking to meet, therefore their life is lived limited. It is vital that you share what you learn in this area.

- **Dormancy:** These people don't show up at your doorstep every morning, so don't think you'll come across a new one every other week, it doesn't work like that. Instead, most only appear when there's a major problem in your life or when there is about to be a major shift, advancement or promotion on your journey. Whatever the case, don't be frustrated when you feel like there's no one around to help you, motivate you or guide you. This only means that there are still things that you can do and must do for yourself before the next person or group of people are sent to help take you to the next level.

- **Germination:** Support its growth by accepting your position as a part of someone else's destiny team to encourage, motivate, and assist them. Also, awareness is the golden key to a lot in life, so the more you practice being aware in all things, the more every seed will grow immeasurably in your life.

Kalamazoo, Michigan

United States of America

"Greatness is the ability to embrace failure, knowing that the failure doesn't mean stop altogether. Failure simply requires an examination of the current process and making a change. Greatness is also about being able to allow others to fail, letting them fail—rather than doing for them—and then mentoring with kindness and grace. Failure is nothing more than a step on the path toward success and one can have many failures before success occurs. Thomas Edison and Abraham Lincoln were experts in failure and yet their successes still stand the test of time."

-Dr. Diana Stout

Writer | Associate Department Chair Davenport University

2:50pm - Time to be Great.

Hyderabad Andhra Pradesh
India

"To me greatness is a clarity; a bliss not necessarily reflected in wealth or richness. It is sublime feeling and I believe the unconscionable will never know of it. It is simply a toss between "right" and "wrong". When you listen to that small voice and go with it, you feel great. That's it. And then you get to be happy and have great fun as well!"

-Raj Viswanadha

Author | Children's Writer

Los Angeles, California
United States of America

"Greatness as a leader comes when a clear vision of the future is expressed in terms that others understand and embrace in carrying out the mission to achieve that future."

-John Morris

Vistage Chair | Mentor for CEO Peer Groups

Malawi

"I believe that if I conceptualize something and then with my effort make that concept real, then I am great!"

-Augustine Mumba

Associate Currency Trader at Chasefu Trading

BE BOLD.

Greatness doesn't have to include all. Instead it separates for a purpose. That purpose is to lead.

Miami, Florida
United States of America

"Greatness is giving the very best of yourself everyday regardless of the situation. It is offering an act of kindness to someone in need without requiring recognition from others. Greatness is knowing deep down inside -- the only person you need to impress is you."

-Dr. Cindy M. Cork

CEO at Riches Thru Health LLC

Jerusalem
Palestine

"Greatness is the ability to smile while your eyes are filled with tears, to rise up after failure and to give without expecting anything in return."

-Majd Nabut

CEO of J&S Trading Group

10:23am - Time to be Great.

New York, New York
United States of America

"Greatness is to rise above one's ego & mediocrity of one's life, to reach the ultimate level of the soul's journey to learn one's purposeful life lesson on earth."

-Lz Franchini

Creator/Co-Owner/Executive Producer at A G Production LLC

Seed 29
SET THE STAGE

SET THE STAGE

Are you ready for your life today? Are you doing the

necessary things needed to make the next hour, day, week, month or year better for yourself? In life we have two choices: one is to do nothing, the other is to set the stage. Most people are doing one or the other. The process and longevity of preparation can be grueling, depressing and down right draining, but it still has to be done. Nothing is promised, nor is much for certain these days. Setting the stage for what you want to see, hear, accomplish, receive, heal, give, and/or experience in life is mandatory and can ultimately lead you to that place of fulfillment. Some may call you a dreamer, too optimistic, or even say you're living in an imaginary world. Let them remain in the realm of non-existence because that's exactly how they appear to the world of movers & shakers and achievers. Prepare for you. Get your ducks in order for yourself. It's not selfish, it's absolutely eminent if you want a life of success. Only listen to those with wisdom, knowledge and understanding. Stop wasting your time with small-minded and sometimes no-minded people. Yes you can love them as human beings but you don't have to live like them. Set the stage for your life, then get ready for an amazing journey of time-sensitive reinventions and continual life debuts.

- **Seed Description:** Write, direct, and produce the life you want to live.

- **Soil:** Plant this into your goals, dreams and future.

- **Water:** Water this seed by stopping, taking a moment to decide and write down what all you want to see, do, become, and accomplish during the rest of your life.

- **Oxygen:** Look at life as most films are produced, creating and preparing from the end to the beginning so you'll know exactly what you're aiming for as far as the finished product.

- **Temperature:** There are times when you'll have to readjust, add a few people, remove some, switch directions or even rewrite some parts of your life to continue on the path of greatness set before you. This is normal, just be bold enough to make those decisions when the time comes.

- **Light/Darkness:** Those around you will create light or darkness for this seed so be sure you evaluate your circle of friends and colleagues constantly. You will need more people of light than darkness, those who help guide, motivate and push you to press on. You can't see the stage without light.

- **Dormancy:** This seed rarely experiences dormancy, even through dark seasons, things are being worked on for the premiere revealing in the seasons to come.

- **Germination:** Support its growth by inviting others to be a part of your life production, giving people an opportunity to showcase their best life and set their own stage will always make you greater and cause this seed to produce more of the same.

Woodbridge, Virginia
United States of America

"Greatness to me is the ability to make a difference in individual lives without trying. For it is the things we do out of passion and love that produce greatness."

-Shondra C. Brown Hawkes

Event Experience Producer & Designer

Slovenia

"Greatness is what I would like my sons to think about my life when I'm gone. Knowing that Greatness isn't anything more than the capacity of always trying to be happy through: never-ending self discovery, never-ending compassion to one and others, and never-ending gratefulness."

-Jose Antonio Morales

Entrepreneur

San Antonio, Texas

United States of America

"Greatness is the ability to produce legally and ethically the most goods and services for the most generations with the least amount of resources and no harm to the environment."

-Paul Muljadi

Electrical Engineer

BE WISE.

In the midst of day to day living, we are unaware of our time frame left. Knowing this, you should always be preparing for the next opportunity to expand or reinvent your legacy.

Colombia

"Greatness is when you understand what your purpose in life is."

-Juan Pablo Gaviria

Chief Entertainment Officer at 360 Digital Co

Chicago, Illinois

United States of America

"Greatness is achieved when one's God-given talents are developed to their fullest extent and used according to His will."

-Cecil Archbold Jr.

Voice Actor CecilVoice!

Zimbabwe

"I desire more to serve the poor than to rule. I desire more to make the world a better place for me and the generations to come than to be content in its flaws. I desire more to follow the conviction I have in my heart despite ruthless opposition from belittled minds and closed-in perceptions. I desire to serve God and carry out His will through me for Human kind. I desire to build up those around me and make them realize their full potentials. That is Greatness to me. Using what is in you to do GOOD."

-Milton Kudzai Murongazvombo

CEO Milton Group

Atlanta, Georgia
United States of America

"Greatness is making the decision to seek out your calling, and to be true to it, even when it seems out of reach, when opposition is high, and when a mountain of societal "shoulds" overshadow you. It is waking up every morning, knowing that you are in the exact center of the purpose that called your soul into being at this time, and in this place. It is living, every day, in the center of your God-ordained life mission. Greatness is coming to the end of this life, and being able to say "I did what I came here to do."

-Nicole Dunbar

"The Success Blocker Coach"

Founder of Congruency Incorporated

Seed 30

THE SHOW MUST GO ON

THE SHOW MUST GO ON

The world doesn't stop just because you do. Life continues daily whether we participate or not. You have to make up in your mind right now that you will continue no matter what. No one ever promised life would be perfect or easy. There's no guarantee that others will support your decisions or pursuits. You are you. You have one lifetime to learn to love yourself, respect yourself, and decide that you will do what you need to do, in spite of everything and anyone else that doesn't follow suit. Always continue. The show must go on. As long as time keeps ticking, you need to keep going. Yes, some may hate you, talk badly about you, but the show must go on. Lovers may hurt you, friends may betray you, but the show must go on. Goals may not be accomplished on the first try, dreams may take longer to realize, but the show must go on. The most successful people in the world are those that continued.

- **Seed Description:** Continue life, pursue greatness.

- **Soil:** Plant this seed into every moment of heartache, doubt and those times when you want to stop, throw in the towel and give up. Those days where nothing seems to be going right and when you wonder if those around you are there for you or for something else.

- **Water:** Water this seed encouraging yourself in the midst of that which tries to slow you down or stop you. It must become your mandated daily regimen to motivate yourself.

- **Oxygen:** Understand that life is a journey, a series of destinations, not just life and death. Realize that each day you have the opportunity to experience things and learn from them, this is the road to greatness. By continuing with what you have learned and maintaining a teachable and curious spirit, limits will no longer exist and nothing will be able to hinder your growth.

- **Temperature:** It's not easy keeping a progressive mindset in the midst of those who live only according to what they see and hear. You must communicate with the inspired power within you, this is how you will overcome the doubters and visionless individuals that you are bound to cross paths with or even have to live with for the time being.

- **Light/Darkness:** Greatness is not a popular pursuit, which means those who pursue that realm are a part of a new and extraordinary minority. This presents its own set of issues however, creating solitude and isolation at the highest degree. Your focus must remain steadfast as you continue. You are not like everyone else, no matter who much you try to fit in and claim you are. You were called to stand out, to lead, to change, to innovate, to present ideas, to uplift, to be the light where darkness once had dominion.

- **Dormancy:** Your dormancy days must come to an end with this seed. At some point, hopefully sooner than later, the option of stopping or giving must be erased for good. There should be times of rest but nothing more than that.

- **Germination:** Support its growth by making a life decision to rock life to the fullest. Find those who think and live with the same mindset, attitude and conviction. Each day you awake must serve as confirmation that you must continue and there's more to be accomplished.

Dominica

"Greatness is the ultimate humbling experience and acceptance that "it is not about me". It is in the empathy we feel for others, it is in being present in each moment and having the ultimate experience of living and allowing others to also experience the connectivity to the universe through us. Greatness is knowing who we are, and living our truth honestly and confidently. It is accepting life's challenges with our chins up, face in the wind and knowing that we will fall down and we will rise up again more victorious, stronger, happier and determined. Greatness is living "on purpose" and deliberately."

-Kathlyn Robinson-Pond

CER & Quality Assurance Specialist at Fine Foods Inc
Real Foods Inc

Malmo
Sweden

"Greatness is what you will achieve when working with the best team on something you are really passionate about. You will also need a bit of luck, since even the greatest ideas and start-ups fail sometimes."

-Alex Esser

Entrepreneur | Tunaspot CEO

New York, New York

United States of America

"What is greatness but a state of mind? To define greatness of a parent, a teacher, a coach, a mentor, a sibling, a boss, or a friend, devalues the human experience. To be great is to embrace your whole self, flaws and all. Greatness is the living an honest and true life without reservation."

-Richard Dedor

Communications and Management Specialist | Keynote Speaker

Puerto Varas
Chile

"Greatness is achieving excellence, achieving extraordinary acts of high value, and doing so with a generous heart."

-Jimmy Langman

Editor of Patagon Journal

BE GREAT.

To master patience is to find peace with timing.

Westlake Village, California
United States of America

"Greatness is the ability to end each day feeling you have striven to accomplish your own personal goals, but have also focused on helping others achieve theirs. Greatness is the ability to find daily positivity and be happy with who you are."

-Diane "Di" Krehbiel

Chief Happiness Officer DKKD Staffing

Gambia

"Greatness is the ability to feel a like hero, dream and believe with passion."

-Olami Idowu Lekh

Producer/Director

Jamaica

"Greatness is a gift, but unlike most other gifts, you have to work for it. It is a gift we give ourselves, through our own discipline, perseverance and love for success. It is a gift that frees us from limitations."

-Wayne Blackwood

Student University of the West Indies

Los Angeles, California
United States of America

"Greatness is the ability to end each day feeling you have striven to accomplish your own personal goals, but have also focused on helping others achieve theirs. Greatness is the ability to find daily positivity and be happy with who you are."

-Cheri Valentine

Owner of Handmade Love

Seed 31

CHANGE YOUR
ATMOSPHERE

CHANGE YOUR ATMOSPHERE

We are all surrounded by things and people. Everything and everyone that you come across creates an atmosphere. Be it good or bad, happy or sad, these external atmospheres are a part of life and an almost tangible reality. Be observant and alert. They can determine or influence the way you feel, react and live. It's important to know that you can easily become or change into what you surround yourself with. Knowing this, especially if you are in a situation where your surroundings are negative and you have to remain there for at least now, you will have to rely on creating a positive atmosphere within yourself. Your internal world is the most powerful place you will ever visit. This is easier said than done but it is pivotal for greatness.

- **Seed Description:** Proactively create a positive atmosphere within yourself.

- **Soil:** Plant this into moments of doubt, tragedy, distress, turmoil, heartache or whenever you need to be uplifted and encouraged.

- **Water:** Water this seed by observing the way certain things and certain people make you feel. Pay attention to what makes you upset and that which makes you full of joy. Use this research and information to create reserves of inner power to better help you deal with situations and people who you'd rather not deal with at all.

- **Oxygen:** Surround yourself with only uplifting things, music, and people, that impart peace, progress, productivity, joy and love into your life

- **Temperature:** Unfortunately, in today's society, there are several things presented daily that aim to bring us down, make us worry, cry, fear and feel inadequate. It's not easy remaining positive through it all but at this point, at this moment in human existence, we have to do all we can to live above the chaos and negativity that our world loves to glorify. It is your duty to not only think great but to live it out as well.

- **Light/Darkness:** The beauty of this seed is that it can change your life forever. It also allows you to see things differently, look at life with a fresh perspective and ignore nonsense. On the downside of it, some will dislike you because they don't embody the same perspective.

- **Dormancy:** It times of dormancy when you could care less about being positive within, and believe me, we all have those moments, just remember that there is no turning back and that you can only downgrade from this point. Once you've truly tasted and experienced greatness within your soul, attitude, ideas and spirit, nothing else but greatness will satisfy.

- **Germination:** Support its growth by using this seed as often as you can. It takes practice to fully cultivate this one. It doesn't happen overnight. It may take several seasons until ripe. The more you use this seed, the greater it will grow and manifest automatically in your life.

12:31am - Time to be Great.

Minneapolis, Minnesota

United States of America

"Greatness is reaching inside of yourself and pulling the best of what's inside of you out. Greatness is persevering against all odds. Greatness is believing in someone when they do not believe in themselves. Greatness is when your works validate your words."

-A.J. Briscoe

Owner | Author | Operator at Stomp Entertainment

Island of Malta

"Greatness is a measure of one's ability to understand and love others."

-Brian Role'

International Magician and Illusionist

Cyprus

"Greatness is the ability to pursue and believe in your potential, especially where everyone sees none in you."

-Nothando Moyo

Ph. D, Founder Moxies Beauty Parlour

Auckland
New Zealand

"Greatness is a state of growing, self discovery, being yourself and being the best! How are you? I am GREAT!"

-Pavel Laletin

CEO Game of Startups

BE BOLD.

It is our earthly and divine responsibility to help someone in our lifetime.

Salinas, California
United States of America

"Greatness is to understand yourself, to take control of your mind. Greatness is a person who can take a bad situation and turn it into a good one. One who thinks outside the box and then makes their own box. The sky has no limit, the same goes for your life."

-Chris Narez

Realtor

Iceland

"Greatness is Life and nature."

-Thorunn Reynisdottir

CCO IcelandREPS

Chicago, Illinois
United States of America

"To me greatness means to discover the inner intuition, that voice of strength that processes the essence of what you were fortune to be. Each finger print denotes uniqueness that's in each of us, to bring into fruition our predestined purpose!"

-Lenear "Royalty" Harris

Artist | Audio Post | Videography

Fort Lauderdale, Florida
United States of America

"Greatness is helping another in their time of need whether you like that person or not. It is the ability to put your ego aside and do the right thing for another human being."

-Brooklyn Murphy

Actress

Seed 32
THE JOURNEY

THE JOURNEY

One of the most important things to learn in your lifetime is to appreciate the journey of your life. Every day, every experience, the highs and lows, the new and the old. As you seek to become and achieve, it will all seem useless and unfulfilling unless you are aware and observant of the journey taken to get there. When aware of the journey, you become one with your goal. Remain open and teachable because surprises often greet us along the way. There is so much to learn, endless things to see and more than enough fascinating people to meet. Don't settle for the prize only, take authority over the journey. When you do, more life will be added to you and your value to the world will be increased. Invite the journey with open arms, then let life throw you the biggest party ever.

- **Seed Description:** Awareness of your life journey.

- **Soil:** Plant this into moments and seasons of life that are significant to you.

- **Water:** Observation waters this seed. So many live without ever taking notes of the multiple things happening in them and around them. You can't appreciate your life if you don't pay attention to it.

- **Oxygen:** We only have so much time alive to actually enjoy life. The majority spend most of it working or working towards something for a long period of time, then use the remaining years to create some sense of happiness out of our decisions. We must learn to let everything be a part of the journey, even that which we work toward. Waiting for the future outcome to begin enjoying and observing life is the saddest thing imaginable. Life is now, no matter what it involves, it always now.

- **Temperature:** Genuine happiness comes from within. It is found within the innermost parts of you and is manifested through a knowing and loving of yourself. This journey of life has no guarantees so you can never rely on the journey for your happiness. There may be things or people that make you happy, but authentic happiness must be birthed within you even before you acknowledge the journey.

- **Light/Darkness:** Your life journey is always on display for others to see. People watch each other, whether they tell you or not, somebody is watching. None of us are perfect but for those of us who desire to live in our greatness, we must pursue our most perfect presentation. No, do not appear to be something you aren't, only be the very best you can be and just be real about it, about everything. Laziness, doubts, double-mindedness and an unteachable spirit will always cause you to make a wrong turn during the journey or get off the path completely. Life isn't long enough anymore to make up for lost time.

- **Dormancy:** At the right age, which could be any age, depending on the maturity of your spirit, life awareness will introduce itself to you. For some, like myself, it was as early as the teenage years, for others it may be later on in life. When it does arrive, you must make a choice then to listen and follow. Dormancy after this moment can cause you to miss your mission and your purpose in life, plus multiple destinations and several other opportunities that were awaiting you. I do believe you can regain it if you get back on track fast enough, however, the longer this seed remains dormant, the greater chances for mediocrity to become your best friend.

- **Germination:** Support its growth by giving attention to inner promptings and instincts, by witness changes, growth and opportunities each year, by making sure you plan as well as live in the moment, not just for you but for others who are observing your journey as well.

New York, New York
United States of America

"Simply put, greatness is about developing conscious awareness of your own intrinsic attributes and your own dreams - then using your attributes to achieve your dreams."

-Chris Camden

Founder at Rocketing Corporation

Copenhagen
Denmark

"Greatness is when you go beyond your own, your families or friends expectations."

-Michel Diederichsen

Entrepreneur

Chicago, Illinois
United States of America

"1. Greatness is being able to look in the mirror and love the person looking back at you! 2. Greatness is being a "Doer" not a "Talker" 3. Greatness is when what is fulfilling to you is also fulfilling and enlightening to others."

-Xavia Fox

Exec. Producer/Host of the "Xavia Fox Talks" Show

BE WISE.

Approach success with wisdom and balance. Wisdom to help you discern that which is authentic and those around you who are genuine. Balance to help you properly measure the cost against the reward, so that you come out lacking nothing, without regret, yet instead with gratitude and the right spirit to share your experience and your new insight.

Riga
Latvia

"Greatness is the ability to recognize your strengths and use them for unselfish purposes, especially if it isn't the easiest path to go."

-Guntis Coders

CEO Walmoo

Memphis, Tennessee
United States of America

"Greatness is being humble enough to own your mistakes and turn them into good. Greatness comes in the knowing that hard work and dedication pays off. Greatness happens when we don't need to work to be motivated. Greatness is embracing the wisdom of others. Greatness is knowing that your success not only depends on the people who are a blessing to you, but the blessing that you are to others."

-Kaye Thompson

Owner at Global Advance Virtual Assistance

Saudi Arabia

"Greatness is the ability to make a positive difference and contribution to yourself, the people around you, your family, your Country, your Nation, and to the whole world."

-Mohsen Almajnouni

Saudi Arabia Refining and Petrochemical Leaders

Austin, Texas

United States of America

"Greatness is a lifetime investment of believing in oneself, and putting in the work to become (or create) something truly considered "Great." Each of us, in our own unique and personal way, can bring more good into this world. We can positively affect other people during our own lifetimes, and hopefully beyond, simply (and most difficulty) by allowing ourselves to truly be who we are. With a lifetime of effort, education, experience, sharing and sacrifice, we can each achieve things which we regard as Great. Be it Athletic or Musical, Analytical or Philosophical, by sharing and developing our talents and abilities with others, we can achieve so much more than without that effort and sacrifice."

-Jei Gaither

Seasoned iOS | Multimedia Developer

Seed 33
A FOCUSED LIFE

A FOCUSED LIFE

There are only 24 hours in a day and sadly only 7 days in a week. Do you ever wish you had more time? Wouldn't it be nice to have more weekend days to relax and regroup? Since the beginning of time life has gotten shorter and shorter. Years go by like weeks and weeks like minutes. We should be wise to capitalize on right now. Your life is all you have and no one other than Almighty God knows how much longer you have to live it. Don't waste time wasting time. I'm sure you've heard people say "Don't take life so seriously". That's one of the most ridiculous things you can ever tell another living soul. Life is serious. It is a gift and one that should be used to its full potential. Yes there are situations in life that you shouldn't take so seriously but life itself, you should. This is your life. You only have one. Pray, plan and prepare for everything you want, take everyday serious. It doesn't matter if you're working or resting, it's all a part of who you are and what you shall become. Ask God for vision, seek out your purpose, live life and become a part of the few who wake up with passion and expectation. For those who don't take their life as serious, I'm really not sure why they are here.

- **Seed Description:** Live a focused life.

- **Soil:** Plant this into everyday life, even times of relaxation and rejuvenation.

- **Water:** Water this seed by staying centered on who you are and who you desire to become.

- **Oxygen:** Investigate your skills, passions, dislikes, likes, wants, desires. These all help you discover more about yourself so you're able to have more direction and answers when it comes to what you'd like to see in the present and future.

- **Temperature:** Distractions are at an all time high in the world we now live in. Most will probably come from those closest to you. You will have to decide the best way to approach and handle this. some gently, others aggressively. You cannot waste a lot of time in this area.

- **Light/Darkness:** You will quickly notice the difference between yourself and plenty of others when you apply this seed. This is not to say you are better than anyone else but it is to say that it will be obvious as to who is focused and who isn't. Your goal is to continue and at the same time, motivate and assist others who truly desire to take their life up a notch.

- **Dormancy:** There are no dormant moments for this seed. There are times when you may think "Is it all worth it?", but that's normal and expected. True enough, we are born, we work, we pursue, we die. I've asked the question to myself and God several times yet my personal answer remains the same, "It needs to be done and I'm the one to do it."

- **Germination:** Support its growth by using your time wisely, planning and keeping a more organized schedule as to what and who you dedicate and share your time with.

Marin County, California
United States of America

"Greatness is the act of sharing your life essence with others: partners, family, neighbors, community, colleagues, co-workers. It is waking up everyday asking yourself, "How can I inspire the life of another today?" And then doing it! Greatness is accepting the failure along with the successes as part of this beautiful experience we are having as spirits in a human body. It's teaching others how to plant and grow their own food. Greatness is teaching others how to read and supporting women's literacy worldwide. Greatness is speaking your Truth, standing up for what is right and just. Greatness is what you are here to be and do."

-Shera Sever

Organizational Strategist | Speaker | Author
Career/Life Coach

Drogheda
Ireland

"Greatness is talents, quality and skills that someone has. Even though they may go through obstacles and challenges in life, they still stand strong no matter the situations."

-Hayate Dehil

Artist Development

Port Orchard, Washington
United States of America

"Greatness is being able to accept the image reflected in your mirror while being a positive and productive example to the people watchers of this world."

-Michael E. Simpkins

Director of Operations NCS Training

Serbia

"Greatness is when you have nothing and you still give."

-Danijela Vujisic

Professor Italian Language at European University Belgrade

BE GREAT.

Without any expectation, loving all humans is Greatness. Being the same in all situations of life, whether it is happiness or sorrow, that is Greatness.

Duluth, Georgia
United States of America

"Greatness is the understanding of the purpose, the plan, and the place or person of your Godly assignment. In order to obtain that greatness it requires clarity from God, which is the Purpose; to be in compliance with God, which is the plan; and consistency with God, which is the place or person. Being able to see the spiritual growth and positive changes in others and yourself through your journey is greatness in itself. "

-April McNair

CEO ALMs Management Group

Kaunas
Lithuania

"Greatness for me is giving your best on a constant basis and staying truly happy about it."

-Tomas Pagirys

Entrepreneur

Perrysburg, Ohio

United States of America

"Greatness is reaching one's full potential of becoming the person that you are designed to become and igniting that full potential within everyone with whom you come in contact. It is running to the finish line in every situation with all of your effort and never looking back with regrets."

-Jennifer Glacken

President/CEO Glacken Health & Wellness

Seed 34
CELEBRATE YOU

CELEBRATE YOU

You are a wonderful creation. You are a living spectacle. You are a genius. How often do you hear those things about yourself? Not everyday I assume. Society has succumb to such mediocre living and thinking to where we have truly ignored the value of not only who we are but also who created us. Truth will always set you free and bring you to a higher level thinking. It is important that you celebrate you and love the you that sometimes others fail to acknowledge. There isn't much you can do for or teach people when you haven't done for or taught yourself. Self-love and self-celebration prepares you to be love to the world. A happy you will always work towards producing happiness in others. Happy people would rather not hang around down and depressed individuals unless the purpose is to influence and change that negative atmosphere. Celebrating you for you removes all the facades of what the world tells you to celebrate. It gives you strength, hope, endurance and most importantly, appreciation for yourself.

- **Seed Description:** Celebrate you and your journey of life.

- **Soil:** Plant this into situations and moments when things don't seem to go the way you want them. Know that you are still amazing, you must continue, and that it's just a part of the journey.

- **Water:** When you make small or large progress and accomplishments, take a moment to make notice of it. It's ok to blow your own horn every now and then. Find a way to reward yourself for completing goals and tasks.

- **Oxygen:** This seed requires that you breathe more life, time and focus into the good things about you and not so much into the things that you don't like about yourself.

- **Temperature:** Many people are unhappy with their lives, so telling someone to celebrate themselves is risky. The key to this seed is to get to know yourself first and foremost. You can't possibly celebrate yourself when you barely know who you are. It is mandatory that you establish a relationship with self, the person within, so that you don't miss out on some of the most important communication of all, that which is shared between your inner voice and instinct.

- **Light/Darkness:** Be wise when you celebrate yourself publicly. Of course not everyone around you wants you to be celebrated, sad but true. If publicly, it's best to celebrate yourself with those who genuinely care about you. When they aren't available then you find ways to celebrate and reward yourself solo. Disregard those that envy you. The more you live in your greatness, the more obvious it will become of those who truly support you and those who were waiting and hoping for you to fail.

- **Dormancy:** Most people can't throw a party for themselves daily so there will be times of dormancy however, you should still carry yourself daily in a way that represents confidence within and great appreciation for who you are becoming.

- **Germination:** Support its growth by cultivating and enhancing the skills and traits about yourself that you love the most. Also, by becoming more aware of you, you'll be able to notice impressive things about yourself much faster and eventually see that you have been great all along. It was just a matter of time before the evidence was brought before the jury.

2:24pm - Time to be Great.

Chicago, Illinois
United States of America

"Greatness is going above all obstacles including yourself to create and obtain the lifelong dream you never knew you had."

-Taya Elery

CEO Taya Elery Consulting | Virtual Associate

Hiroshima
Japan

"Greatness is to be influential with someone's way of life".

-Hiroyuki Matsumoto

Taxation Consultant

Phoenix, Arizona

United States of America

"Greatness is a measure of your self-worth; consequently, it is a destiny achieved in its highest form. No matter where you are in life, you should be striving to be better. Therefore greatness can only be achieved by the value you place on yourself. Greatness allows you to be willing to go that one step further to be the person that our "Creator" chose us to be. My quote to the world is: If excellence is on your radar, disable mediocrity. Let your best be your best."

-Patrice Register

CEO | Author | Inspirational Thought Leader

Toronto, Ontario
Canada

"Greatness is going to bed at night saying we've done something wonderful. Live with passion and positive energy. Follow your heart."

-Shadi Hagag

CEO Trans-Plan Inc.

BE BOLD.

We open ourselves up for failure, depression, hatred, ignorance and death when we allow an unteachable spirit to live and breathe within us.

Khartoum

Sudan

"Greatness is to be able to understand exactly what is needed to deliver value to humanity and work upon that."

-Omer Ibrahim

BPM Manager Zain Telecom

Libya

"Greatness is when you could be at the expectation of others when they are in lack of resourcefulness, when you could proceed giving and giving without waiting for getting back."

-Mohammed Shakshek

Student at Bangor University

Manama
Bahrain

*"Greatness is having the moral conviction to do what is just
and fair, as against what others may expect you to do."*

-Wasif Ijlal

Co-Head of Asset Management Ithmaar Bank B.S.C.

Malawi

"Greatness is Love! To love people, to be loved and most importantly to LOVE the designer and creator of the Universe, GOD!!"

-Chipha Bwanali

Partner at Cyber Info Tek Ltd

Seed 35
SOMEONE HAS TO DO IT

SOMEONE HAS TO DO IT

Life is a one-time experience and you only get one shot to do what you need to do. Sometimes you may feel like your dreams or visions are too big to accomplish. Some things may seem hard to comprehend as to how it will get done or who is capable of making it happen. I declare to you that you are the one. Most people have doubts and uncertainties, so it's normal in a sense, but the desires and passions within you were placed there for a purpose. This purpose is just for you, therefore it's your responsibility to seek it out and fulfill it. The world is in need of someone authentic, someone who lives a notch above the norm. You are that someone. Don't allow fear to hold you back from taking risks. Someone has to do it.

- **Seed Description:** You are the answer.

- **Soil:** Plant this into days throughout life when you know that you are the person of the moment to make something happen in a certain situation.

- **Water:** Water this seed by perfecting who you are and being aware of what you bring to the table.

- **Oxygen:** Use curiosity to enhance your senses and knowledge of new things. This helps empower you and expand everything within you.

- **Temperature:** Master who you are. This is the passport to greatness.

- **Light/Darkness:** I believe we all have greatness inside of us but not everyone is aware of it, therefore not everyone will recognize it when they see it. You are responsible for releasing your own greatness in your lifetime. It is imperative that you become the ultimate you regardless of who remains blind around you.

- **Dormancy:** You aren't a superhero so never think you are the answer to everything and everyone. There will be times of dormancy but this is only because we all carry different gifts for different situations, centuries, moments and eras. You can only operate where you were gifted to. We were created to fit and produce with individual specialties that create global progress for mankind.

- **Germination:** Support its growth with continual self evaluation. I annually evaluate who I am, what I've learned, who I've become and so forth. It is of extreme importance that you check-in with yourself annually to monitor your progress so you can know what to add in the days and years to come, which increases your value and magnifies your greatness reach.

Des Moines. Iowa

United States of America

"Greatness is to be appreciated for what you are best at. Through sharing your gift, you have influenced others to live their lives doing what they are best at. Greatness may be appreciated or not, but it is always felt."

-Ini Augustine

CEO SocialWise Media Group

Lisbon

Portugal

"You've achieved greatness when every time you wake up in the morning you feel happy to be working on what you dream and be surrounded by everyone who loves you."

-Henrique Gomes

Principal at VoiVoda Ventures

New York, New York
United States of America

"Greatness is mastering yourself. Once you understand your motivation for doing things, for reacting to circumstances and people in certain ways, and realize your true passion, you can change yourself, change your path, and create the future you want. 'Know thyself' and the universe will open up to you."

-J. Anthony Bronston

Entrepreneur | Realtor, Coldwell Banker

BE WISE.

Greatness is not self-sustaining nor everlasting. Time will move forward and the scramble to reach greatness begins again.

Los Angeles, California

United States of America

"Greatness is the ability to be perfected by God's Love, casting out all your fears, so you can in turn, perfectly love others into their own holy-ness. Broken people break people and hurt people hurt people - so when we forgive, it releases our limitless potential. It starts from a renewed mind revelation of who you are in God's Image, giving you power and might to make your dreams come true."

-LeRoy Mobley

Actor | CEO The LeRoy Mobley Company

Kuwait

"Greatness is an absolute discipline possessed by an individual of total self integration. Through right kind of education Greatness can be achieved. By sowing seeds of TRUTH, BEAUTY and LOVE, we can spread greatness."

-Vinod Divakaran

Director at Thanal Maram Foundation

Monze
Zambia

"Greatness is to wash your servant's feet, hug your enemy and give the poor your only remaining plate; it's kindness and humility coated with humbleness."

-Wanderi Jessee

Chairperson Department of Music Rusangu University

Indianapolis, Indiana

United States of America

"Greatness to me is a quality of being distinguished; in such a manner that sets you apart from any and everything that keeps one from succeeding. It is an achievable goal that can be conquered if one can capitalize their full potential. Also, it is a lifestyle that I'm destined to obtain."

-Don Oliver Jr.

CEO/Graphic Engineer Don Marcus Design & Print

Seed 36
SEPARATED TO LEAD

SEPARATED TO LEAD

There is a high price to pay to be a true leader. One that inspires, encourages and has the power to change a life and the spirit of another in one encounter. Such impact power involves a lifelong humbling process. So many people live double if not triple lives. They put on a smile in public while living a sad life behind closed doors. You must know yourself and your Creator to discover the secrets to this life. Peace that passes all understanding, undying hope and the endless abundance of love that can only be tapped through constant communication with God. This seems to have become foreign to several in society but in order to rise above the status quo, you will often have to separate yourself from the way others think. One of your most valuable keys to greatness is the way you think. You may feel alone at times but you must understand that you have been separated in order to lead. Leaders, true leaders, those God positioned throughout time not only thought outside the box, they removed the box completely. It's time for you do the same.

- **Seed Description:** Set apart and designated for a greater purpose.

- **Soil:** Plant this into moments throughout life when you feel the need to withdraw from your normal routine and certain human associations in order to prepare for something greater.

- **Water:** Water this seed by being honest with yourself and what you feel on the inside of you. Listen to that inner voice when it speaks and gives direction, no matter how odd or detached the instructions may appear.

- **Oxygen:** Greatness is individually dispersed throughout segments of life, often during times when you are neutral of others, in seasons and in moments of isolation. It would be wise that you remain observant to receive your upgrades.

- **Temperature:** Being a leader is a sacrifice while also the greatest honor you can ever receive. The power to influence a life in a positive way, to inspire, is one of the greatest forces on the planet. Never take the opportunity to lead for granted.

- **Light/Darkness:** Even though the results of being separated to lead can be great and extremely fulfilling not only for you but several others as well, this high calling often leads to loneliness and detachment. Don't expect to be understood by everyone around you unless they themselves know of your purpose and your sacrifice.

- **Dormancy:** There are no dormant seasons however there will be feelings of dormancy. This is only because during the process of separation, there will be days when solitude appears to be a sign of stagnation but it's not. Solitude should be used to listen to the voice within and to prepare for the next move.

- **Germination:** It helps to find others in the same position to support its growth however, this is easier said than done, but you must still seek them out. In the meantime, use inspiration from other leaders to boost your confidence and moral, identify those things and people that strengthen you the most and keep them close by. Pray for inner peace, wisdom and endurance.

Helsinki
Finland

"Greatness is the ability to win yourself and do what is right and what is great even your body and the entire cognitive system is refusing to do so. Greatness is to show love when there is hate. Greatness is to stand up to make things right and help the weak when everybody else just turns their heads away."

-Cristina Andersson

WinCoach | Author

4:23pm - Time to be Great.

Atlanta, Georgia
United States of America

"Greatness is the wisdom to seek God in the details and the strength to follow what He shows you in them."

-Cassandra Hollis

Film Director and Owner at Holy Hill Films, LLC

Hayward, California
United States of America

"Greatness is having the courage to achieve success by living out your passion, despite all of the obstacles you will face on the journey to reaching your highest potential."

-Bramani Quinn

Owner and Performer of Soul Expressions Fusion Arts (SEFA)

Bhutan

"Greatness is living life to the fullest and doing so contributing in whatever small ways to making the planet a better place for all future generations. You live life only once!"

-Kezang Kezang

Project Coordinator at Department of IT & Telecom

BE GREAT.

We were created to fit and produce with individual specialties that create global progress for mankind.

Houston, Texas

United States of America

"To me, greatness means doing extraordinary things to make a difference in the lives of others. I can honestly say that I feel more alive when I write stories for my media company, Vallano Media, hosting a radio show that allows guests to share their passion with the listeners, that's what greatness is about."

-Cheval John

Founder Vallano Media | Freelance Writer

Blogger and Radio Show Host

Copenhagen

Denmark

"My battle with colon cancer connected me to the universal energy known as God. Andy, our youngest son was only 2 years old when I was diagnosed and had to plan my own death if I was going to die in the near future. I never asked why me, but why now. There was no anger, but a feeling of what do I need to learn? Cancer gave me spiritual insight and opened a door to my inner own greatness. The greatness of getting a 2nd chance and now spending most of my time supporting terminally ill families around the world. Namaste."

-Susan Binau

International Communication and PR Manager

Founder Charities in USA and Denmark

Denver, Colorado
United States of America

"Greatness is the ability to meet raw life head-on and unaided. To meet each day with no fear. No fear of others expectations, of failing, of perceptions, of self doubt, of the unknown. True Greatness is succeeding with the ignorance and joy of a child."

-Enrique Gutierrez

Father | Entrepreneur

Seed 37
UNSEEN POWER

UNSEEN POWER

There is unseen power and forces working on your behalf every single day. The news doesn't report on it, family and friends really never mention it and you probably don't acknowledge it much, but this power remains. Being created from Spirit, which is God, this Spirit continues to do its purpose in your life no matter what. It's in you and all around you. We all have access to witness this power do more in our lives. Everything comes down to whether you want to be connected or disconnected, decide today. This power gives you access to everything and everywhere, it has no limits. The human mind can only comprehend but so much. Don't try to understand it all, just receive it for it has already been placed within you for purposes you can only discover by asking God. (reference Seed 13).

- **Seed Description:** Inner power from the Creator.

- **Soil:** Plant this into tough moments, when days are long, stresses are high and doubts are many.

- **Water:** This power has multiple functions: to heal, comfort, inspire, create, love, teach, motivate, build and more. It is watered every time you operate in any of these.

- **Oxygen:** Accept this power, acknowledge it, and it will open up endless opportunities above and beyond what you pursue in life.

- **Temperature:** Many people live life without any awareness of the life within them. We go and go, day after day, year after year, striving for something that we have no definition for. Now is the time to search within you for your answers and receive the wisdom that awaits your question.

- **Light/Darkness:** Don't run around town talking about your 'inner power', people will surely keep away from you. We have become a race that doesn't expect anything more than what we see. The most powerful forces on Earth are unseen, they can only be expressed or demonstrated.

- **Dormancy:** This power is never dormant, it continues to work even when you sleep. It is activated upon instinct, need, request, and divine intervention.

- **Germination:** Support its growth by asking God to increase it within you, that way you can observe it in operation and learn how to spot it in others. At that point, unite with those to further impact the world as a team

Atlanta, Georgia

United States of America

"Greatness is having the ability to remove the barriers in your life that you are personally responsible for, implementing your dreams while accomplishing your purpose and being able to share and inspire others to do the same!"

-Granville T. Freeman III

CEO N'Spired By Achievement Services & Solutions, LLC.

Jordan

"Greatness is being able to overcome the challenges with a positive attitude and to be able to lead the people around to succeed in reaching their aims with support, passion, with knowledge sharing and collaborative efforts."

-Mohammad Obaidat

AIESEC Alumni

Omaha, Nebraska
United States of America

"Greatness is living fearlessly with ultimate confidence residing in your mind, body, and spirit! Greatness is mastering the skill of focusing on only the task at hand (proactive action in the present) while avoiding disappointing thoughts of past failures and stressful thoughts of a made-up overwhelming future. The key to Greatness is planning the future, as a guide, but living everyday in the focus of prioritized action in the present."

-Brian Nogg

CFO of I-Go Van and Storage Co.,
An Agent for United Van Lines

Nairobi

Kenya

"Greatness is the ability to inspire through acts that would normally be considered ordinary. Quite frankly, it is the ordinary in extraordinary."

-Solomon Maonga

Student

BE BOLD.

Greatness is an achievement in one's life when you have shed all worry, fear, doubt and disbelief and you can just be. You are at peace with the world, with everyone and everything in it and the world sees it. People emulate what they admire.

Chesapeake, Virginia

United States of America

"Greatness is living up to your full potential, and inspiring others to do the same, during extraordinary circumstances."

-Joseph David

President of The Milani Group

Croatia

"Greatness to me means that you have balance in your career, family, health and personal relationship with your friends. When you are a leader it means that you have a big influence on the lives of other people and society and you are the one who helps others to be a better father, better mother, a better friend, a better person.

-Igor Bartolic

System Engineer Senior at Ericsson

Chicago, Illinois
United States of America

"Greatness is when a visionary passionately focuses on creating and implementing a plan to make someone else's vision become a reality."

-Traci Weathers

Co-Owner at Society Girls Shop

Sofia

Bulgaria

"As an artist, Greatness to me is when I am in the state of creating something, as a human Greatness should be when I am in the state of falling in love - with another human, with a piece of art, with an animal or alien, well love in general."

-Anna "Anna Bo" Bocheva

Composer

Seed 38
THE BATTLE OVER YOUR INFLUENCE

THE BATTLE OF YOUR INFLUENCE

There are forces in the spiritual realm that work against you.

Negative powers that not only despise your existence but are even more disturbed by your potential. Your influence alone can change millions of lives, impact the globe and help heal humanity. Take the life of Jesus Christ, by far the most influential and controversial individual to ever walk the Earth. He was undoubtedly hated as well as loved. Though he went about healing the people, feeding many and giving thousands hope and joy, still several wanted him arrested and killed. His influence was undeniable, as it continues globally today. Jesus wasn't doing anything wrong to harm anyone, instead he did the complete opposite but still managed to catch hell from all sides. This goes to show you that even when doing good, there will be those who oppose you. Does it make sense? Of course not but this is our current world system. You must be aware of the powers against you and equally if not more aware of the dominating power within you to continue and to conquer. Be mindful of this, your influence depends on it.

- **Seed Description:** Empower and protect your influence.

- **Soil:** Plant this into your present and future planning. Know that your life alone should be influencing someone in a positive way.

- **Water:** Water this seed by observing as many of those you can who observe you, or at least keeping an ear and eye open to some of the responses or chatter that may arise concerning you. You don't have to know everything that's being said but it's good to obtain a certain amount of info just in case you have to correct the masses when necessary and set the record straight.

- **Oxygen:** Be steadfast in that which you believe in and that which you stand for. Don't waiver once your mind is made up. Sadly, there is a group of people who sit and wait to find fault in others, especially targeting those in the public eye or anyone who has experienced any amount of success.

- **Temperature:** Influence is a powerful and dangerous entity. Being respected and having the power to persuade others comes with its own set of benefits and disadvantages. Know what you're getting into. Welcome boldness and endurance into your life to help you stand your ground in any unfortunate or terrifying situation.

- **Light/Darkness:** Influence is to be used to impact lives, enhance the world, and bring people together to perform impossible tasks that would have never been accomplished otherwise. When it is used to cause harm and bring negativity to society in any way, it turns into wickedness.

- **Dormancy:** You should be aware of this seed at all times. Influential people are influential even when they aren't trying to be.

- **Germination:** Support its growth by awareness of the fact that you are influential. Almost everything you do, say, agree with, disagree with, attend, and even wear can produce influence. Your influence determines your legacy, therefore the more you enhance your influence, the greater your legacy will be.

San Antonio, Texas

United States of America

"Greatness is continuing to love and forgive the people in your life when they fail you. When you can continue to trust and have faith that never waivers and remain calm while carrying on, your path to greatness has begun. Diligently seeking your purpose with a positive attitude shines a light on that path for all to see. Your light of love, forgiveness, strength and positive attitude will become the light which directs others in their journey. Be the example and shine!"

-Lori Sears

Queen of Inspiration at PC Mailing Services

Vellore
India

"Greatness means to keep one's head and heart above the mundane and at the same time remain humbly rooted to the ground realities!"

-Dr. Jameel Shaik

Faculty Vellore Institute of Technology

Atlanta, Georgia

United States of America

"Greatness is recognizing your God-given gifts, talents, and abilities and utilizing them to overcome obstacles, to uplift and encourage others, and to have a positive impact on your world. Greatness starts from within but is an example that is witnessed by others."

-C. Nathaniel Brown

Writer | CEO of Expected End Entertainment

Salerno
Italy

"Greatness for me is Love, people who love you! Every single day you must feel light. I feel light when I see my wife's eyes! Greatness is all for that, Greatness is my life."

-Carmine Cavaliere

Owner at Carmine Cavaliere Servizi Legali/Legal Service

BE WISE.

Learn what you can from those who have already walked the path. Don't make your life any harder or more complicated than life already is.

Minneapolis, Minnesota
United States of America

"Greatness is not a description you can give to ideas created by you, but it is a description others can give to ideas created by you."

-Jeffry 'Jeff' Brown

Executive Coach | Strategist

Vienna
Austria

"Greatness is ones ability to conceptually perceive & achieve."

-TJ Hicks

CEO/Producer at Minimalsoul

4:04pm - Time to be Great.

Orange Country, California
United States of America

"Greatness is the amount of joy and satisfaction you achieve in your life and the lives of others by understanding the unique gifts and talents you've been given, and applying them to the life you live."

-Scott A. Shuford

Chief Engagement Officer FrontGate Media

Seed 39

DIVINE CONNECTIONS

DIVINE CONNECTIONS

$\mathscr{I}$ believe there are angels among us. No not the ones all dressed in white with wings and glistening eyes but instead angels in human form. Some are knowingly sent by God to help people while others are here without knowing they are sent. Sounds strange to some but from my observation, I continue to find this to be true, at least for me. Some things in life just happen but there are other times when you know a fact that something or someone miraculously stepped in on your behalf to help you. It could be anything, from an almost car wreck to getting a job or promotion you know you aren't qualified for, to a stranger giving you money that you desperately needed, to being healed of a said-to-be incurable disease after an encounter with someone. Some people are sent and placed into your life to help take you higher. Are these just regular everyday people? I don't think so. Many are divine connections. They are set apart, just for you, for specific moments. We all have them but very few know how to take full advantage of their existence. You must expect something great to happen plus be a pursuer of your purpose, dreams and destinies in life. This shows the Creator that you want to be here and that you appreciate His investment in you. You'll soon witness and realize more divine connections and supernatural moments in your life.

- **Seed Description:** Awareness of supernatural help throughout life.

- **Soil:** Plant this into your daily life, expecting miracles.

- **Water:** Water this seed by opening your mind to the fact we were created and didn't just appear or evolve. We are greater than what our minds have been taught and we have access to more than what we see.

- **Oxygen:** Observe everything, everyone, everywhere. We tend to miss out on many secrets, extraordinary occurrences and valuable wisdom during life because of our casual approach.

- **Temperature:** The media has been successful in making it appear as if the world doesn't care about the divine or supernatural happenings. There are so many things happening around the world that would leave anyone in pure awe yet these things rarely become top news stories. Interesting I say. Don't let popular media detour you from experiencing a higher life, one that involves a greater awareness of spiritual things and discernment of why the media chooses to ignore it in the first place. Be self-motivated and encourage yourself, not letting the global airwaves distract you with negativity every single day.

- **Light/Darkness:** Expect several people to think you're crazy if you mention angels or anything related to the supernatural. Many people have been deceived and lost touch with their own inner power or any potential power from another source. Use what you know to your advantage, then let the amazing things that occur in your life speak for themselves because they surely will, as they continue to do in mine.

- **Dormancy:** This seed only experiences dormancy when you don't live in the atmosphere of expectancy. Be aware that anything can happen, at anytime, to advance you, enhance your life and make you even greater. Take the limits off of whatever you thought you knew. Welcome a new mindset that believes in miracles.

- **Germination:** Support its growth by making mental notes when you experience amazing things in life. You can even write them down for future reference as well, providing privileged information for someone to review in the future. Remembering the extraordinary things that happen in your life encourages your faith to believe in what can happen again and what new things are possible. Limits do not exist to those who believe.

Denver, Colorado
United States of America

"Greatness can be the common life well lived, doing the ordinary, small things with great care, as spiritual exercises, doing them for the greater glory of God."

-John S. Wren

Founder & CEO at Small Business Chamber of Commerce

London, England

United Kingdom

"Greatness is persevering with and achieving your ambitions, whilst remaining humble and treating everyone as equals."

-Sophie Bowman

Company Director Hypeglo Ltd

Miami, Florida

United States of America

"True greatness is the ability to be consistent in your progression against all odds."

-Barry Pierre

Founder and CEO Abstract Music

BE GREAT.

Arise knowing that you have the power to make the day what it shall be and that your presence will enhance someone else's day as well.

Toronto, Ontario
Canada

"Greatness is the ability to be the best example for others. It means you keep getting up! Regardless!"

-George Fiala

President/CEO Brainwerx Group

Nashville, Tennessee

United States of America

"Greatness is knowing that there is a God and that it is not you. Knowing that success in this life is really not guided by what you do or who you know. It's loving without conditions and speaking "Life" to the hopeless. Not taking anything or anyone for granted."

-Navita Gunter

Vice-Chair at Tennessee Cancer Coalition

Ghana

"Greatness is a much desired attribute everyone would love to have. Greatness compliments an achievement and success. To everyone is given a seed of greatness but the fruitfulness and the growth of such seed depends on individual strength, priority, motivation, purpose and understanding towards life. Greatness indeed feels good to associate with fulfillment. Greatness gives one the edge to offer a helping hand to others. As a believer of the gospel of Christ I believe greatness in profoundly expressed in Christ Jesus."

-Joseph Allotey-Kpakpoe

Jojencon Oil

New York, New York
United States of America

"The Duality of Greatness: Perfection in either road you choose. You can be a servant of Satan, or a servant of Allah (God). Both paths deliver greatness, but only one of these cast its travelers into damnation. Our Creator is Perfect!"

-Philip Muhammad

Film Director | Founder of God's Water Entertainment Foundation

Seed 40

A CLEAR VIEW FROM THE MOUNTAIN

A CLEAR VIEW FROM THE MOUNTAIN

Your greatest assets in life should be getting to know the person within you and who created you. There is an atmosphere of access spiritually, that allows you to hear what others can't hear and see what others can't see. To know why you were born and what you were placed on Earth to do puts you in a privileged class. Your passion is evident and your mission is for certain. Being in this position can only produce greatness and a sure legacy. You have a clear view of your life and with this view, you're able to make present and long-term decisions much easier than most people. It's like being on top of a mountain and looking down to see all the Earth and its creations. With such a view, you have the upper hand in most cases whether you realize it or not. Be thankful for knowing yourself, what you desire, and having a strategy to see it all come to pass. This is an attribute of a leader. One that can stand in any position and still produce, no matter the circumstances. Protect your knowing, surround your vision with mighty soldiers and never let anyone or anything ever block your view. Your perception and view from the top of the mountain will determine what you know, what others don't know, and what you must leave behind for the world to follow.

- **Seed Description:** Clarity of self, mission and legacy.

- **Soil:** Plant this into daily life as well as future planning.

- **Water:** Water this seed by investing time in you, making yourself greater and more knowledgeable. Spending priceless moments on researching within to find out what makes you happy and what makes you upset. Using this information to discover your mission and life. Decide now what you want to leave behind and what you want others to say of you when your name is mentioned.

- **Oxygen:** It saddens me to see people live day to day without any sure direction, plan or life destination. It's mandatory during your journey of life that you realize that it is a journey you are on, and not just living. Acknowledge the journey and seek more than those have sought around you. Life only becomes life when you decide to live for it and not just live because of it.

- **Temperature:** To me greatness must be activated. Though it would be amazing if everyone would operate on higher levels of love, thinking, productivity and so forth but that's not the case. Being a visionary takes practice and focus. So many want this and that yet very few embody the discipline, desire, patience, work ethic and perseverance it takes to receive it.

- **Light/Darkness:** It's obvious that there are more followers than leaders in the world. Whether this is good or bad, I'm not sure, but I do know we need more leaders. Greatness pushes you to lead in some way, whether at home, around friends, in your community, or in front of the world. With this will come those who disagree with you just to disagree. This should be expected. Use your vision, your clear view from the mountain, to revolutionize the times we live in, to create hope and opportunity that no other generation has ever seen.

- **Dormancy:** You should always seek clarity as to where you are in your life once you come of age to notice the importance of it. It's all about awareness when it comes to the next move, the next step, or the next plan of action. Dormancy is rare because your view is always present.

- **Germination:** Wake up with the determination to be a greater you, to expand who you are and what you know, to discover wisdom and the things you desire to make a part of your life and your legacy. This seed will grow without limits and can produce fruit all over the world, forever.

Milwaukee, Wisconsin
United States of America

"Greatness is a force within yourself. To harness greatness, you have to be selfless and willing go beyond the realms of "normal". For most people, this means doing what's right for others before doing what's right for you."

-Jeneen R. Perkins

Solopreneur | Accountant Eclat Enterprises, LLC

Harderwijk
Netherlands

"I learned from Mother Nature that greatness is equal to the small things. This shows in the fractals. This knowledge means that my life and actions and thoughts are inextricably linked and part of it ALL, part of all Greatness."

-Christa de Leeuw van Weenen

CEO Zuss Fashion Design

Belleville, Illinois

United States of America

"Greatness means that as you reflect on your life, in both good times and bad, you see the lessons you have learned as well as the blessings that you have earned along the way."

-Leo Brown

CEO PLB and Fierce Spirituality, Inc.

Senegal

"To be great is only possible if you recognize and reward those people around you that helped you become who you are. You also have to remember to help people that show initiative and enthusiasm, coming behind you to continue to be blessed by those ahead. Greatness is a circle, it's not a straight line. If people respected that, the people they pass going down will be the ones they helped as they were going up. With a straight line, you will pass the people that you stepped on or ignored to get where you wanted to be."

-Sineta George

Owner SenegalStyle Tours

BE BOLD.

Greatness is the ability to create ideas that bring people together to develop something bigger than you.

Dallas, Texas
United States of America

"Greatness is using your spiritual gifts and abilities to support your family, enrich your community and leave behind a legacy of servant leadership."

-Jay Veal

CEO It's Not Complicated Tutoring

Riga
Latvia

"Greatness means the moment of finding the inner harmony and reaching the relaxed state of mind. This is the moment when your soul reads new ideas from the Universe, your cleared and creative mind knows what to do with them, and your relaxed body has enough energy to conquer the goals. The process of achieving the challenges in a way you have decided to act makes you gain new skills and experiences. By using your intuition, open heart and deep sense of doing the things right, Greatness is permanent."

-Raivo Kreicbergs

CEO Rosenso Marcoms

Atlanta, Georgia
United States of America

"Greatness is overcoming the impossible. Taking a dream and making it your own by bringing it to life. Being able to believe in yourself no matter what life throws at you and accomplishing your goal at the end. Greatness is being you."

-Yalonda Edwards

CEO at Youmans Productions Inc

Botswana

"Greatness is far more than the will to be great, it is an emotional instinct that determines the true nature of accepting Failure. Greatness can only be see in the eyes of one that has lost everything but finds that inner heart and power to stand firm and find another way to achieve the goal. It is by far a term but more a hidden uncapped resource that is only found by a few but can be mastered by many if fully understood how to unleash ones instinct to survive."

-Jillian Mary Sigamoney

CEO and Owner of Baratang Holdings & ICanLearnProgram

Seed 41
THE ABUNDANCE MIND

THE ABUNDANCE MIND

As tears flood my eyes, I pray that you will pursue a mind without limits and one that shields itself from mediocre and negative deposits. You are a genius. The creation of you is spectacular in every way. Everything you see and hear around you came from the mind of someone. This mind is endless. Endless in love, peace, hope, long-suffering, kindness, joy, creativity, innovation, ideas, reinvention, faith, inspiration and more. You must replace the mind you once had with the abundance mind. Everything is possible with this mind. Everything is at your fingertips with this mind. Not only does it cause you to think differently, it will also train you to speak with new words and a different voice. Words of direction, affirmation and assurance. A voice of calmness, influence and power.

Limits do not exist. This is the first lesson with the abundance mind. From there, you are immeasurable. Learn, teach, ask questions, explore, seek, take risks, launch into the deep, and discover the mind you were born to have. Don't let what the world define everything you should know. Take authority over your life, present and future. This day is the moment. This moment you must receive the abundance mind.

- **Seed Description:** Think, pursue, and live with a mind of abundance.

- **Soil:** Plant this into your daily life, decisions and moments when you feel the need to settle for less.

- **Water:** Water this seed with action. If you desire more in your life then learn more so that you can pursue more.

- **Oxygen:** Those who think abundantly often surround themselves with the same type of people. Find the abundant thinkers and join their circle. Limits are for the average, abundance is for those without limits.

- **Temperature:** The abundance mind doesn't come cheap or easy. It takes time, education, preparation and dedication to properly develop it and to put it in motion for it to become routine. Great thoughts without action are simply wasted marvels.

- **Light/Darkness:** Your focus must remain on the way you think. Don't even consider what others think about you when concerning this, they do not understand and will never understand unless they open up their lives to the same. Breathe abundance. Speak abundance. Live abundance.

- **Dormancy:** Always flow in the abundance mind. Dormancy has no place in abundance.

Germination: Support its growth by making it a daily habit to feed your new mind of abundance. Study those things and surround yourself with people that enhance the way you think, pursue and live.

Moscow
Russia

"Greatness is to do what you do as good as you can. Then review it and make even better."

-Georgy Saveliev

CBAP

St. Petersburg, Florida
United States of America

"Greatness is found in the successful coalescence of self interest and positive influence."

-Daniel James Scott

Founder Alorum

Dominica

"We only achieve our greatness when we be our very best. Being your best and never settling for less. If you fail, try again and never give up on your goals. Starting over sometimes is not an option but a must. So reach for the stars and achieve your greatness!!!"

-Cheryl Plummer

Owner Real World Atv Rentals and Tours

Los Angeles, California

United States of America

"Greatness is when you are told by someone that at a particular point you had made an indelible positive impact on his/her life and you weren't aware of it at the time. For when you made that impact, your actions were completely pure without intent or manipulation or expectation. Even greater still is being able to tell someone that they made that type of impact on your own life."

-Ron W. Roecker

President and Chief Brand Navigator Enfluence Group

BE WISE.

Being a leader is a sacrifice while also the greatest honor you can ever receive. The power to influence a life in a positive way, to inspire, is one of the greatest forces on the planet. Never take the opportunity to lead for granted.

Bratislava
Slovak Republic

"Greatness is a natural part of life. It is everywhere, we just need to learn to see and feel it."

-Jan Valent

Owner Focus | Freelancer

Cincinnati, Ohio
United States of America

"Greatness to me means the ability to be humble and adaptable in any situation come what may."

-Othello Gooden Jr.

Actor | Writer | Musician

Auckland

New Zealand

"To me, Greatness is first understanding deeply, exactly what YOU want. Not what other people appreciate and respect, not what you want others to think about you but what YOU want. Greatness is firstly understanding that and then doing everything in your power to   achieve it."

-Sam Ovens

Entrepreneur | Marketing & Lead Generation Consultant

Luxembourg

"Greatness is simply the never-ending willingness of a person to learn, grow, achieve and share."

-Ivan Deschamps

Consultant

Seed 42
IF YOU CAN HELP SOMEONE, HELP THEM

IF YOU CAN HELP SOMEONE, HELP THEM

Our world has become a very selfish place to live in. And with this selfishness, those who were already less fortunate have appeared to have gotten worse as far as poverty. I believe there is enough of everything on this planet for all to be fed, clothed, educated and cared for medically. There are no excuses why anyone should have to lack in these important areas of life. You know what you have and what you don't have. You also know to some degree the same about others. It is our earthly and divine responsibility to help someone in our lifetime. Though we may live in different neighborhoods, drive different vehicles, or even eat different foods, still, at the beginning and end of life, we are all the same.

You can accumulate every academic degree known to man, win every award ever created, and be admired by millions but nothing will ever ignite your spirit more than helping another human being when they need it most. It is embedded in us at birth to help. We were born to share, assist and to give. Whether it be time, money, food, clothes, knowledge, or material possessions, we were created givers as is the Creator of all. Applying this to your life will also open assistance from others to you when you need help as well. Give and it shall be given to you. It is amazing the things that can and will happen in your life when you begin helping others.

- **Seed Description:** Help others.

- **Soil:** Plant this into every opportunity where you are able to assist another.

- **Water:** Water this seed by sharing your life.

- **Oxygen:** Our ultimate value is not in our net worth or in our possessions. Our true value is determined by the lives we uplift and enhance in our lifetime.

- **Temperature:** The world has become very selfish. Everyone seems to be out for themselves and the media is quick to show it. You must be the exception. We all need help at some point in life, so you might as well be one of the first to offer it.

- **Light/Darkness:** Being there for someone makes you feel needed and appreciated. Every human being desires those two. The only downside is when someone tries to take advantage of you and misuse your kindness.

- **Dormancy:** Dormancy isn't frequent but there are times when you can't help everyone in every situation. People need assistance in a variety of ways, not just money. The key is to remain open and available, even when you can't help, you can suggest someone or a source that can.

- **Germination:** Support its growth by volunteering for trustworthy nonprofit organizations, using your resources to the fullest to help someone who may not have anyone else and by listening to your heart instead of your mind.

Panama City
Panama

"Greatness is proactivity with a hint of luck."

-Stephanie Lievano

University of Louisville Graduate Student

Canada

"So many people wonder what their 'purpose' is? Try to do at least, one thing for somebody else everyday, your purpose will be defined and so will greatness. When you look back on your life 5, 10, 15 years from now- those will be the moments that you remember. Everything else is window dressing. Keep laughing. Keep swimming."

-Judy Croon

Comedian | Motivational Speaker | Fundraiser

Queens, New York
United States of America

"Greatness is being everything God has called you to be."

-Qasiym Glover

CEO Premium Elderly Care

BE GREAT.

Use your vision, your clear view from the mountain, to revolutionize the times we live in, to create hope and opportunity that no other generation has ever seen.

3:49am - Time to be Great.

Athens

Greece

"Greatness is the simplicity in a complex world."

-Nikos Bogonikolos

President Aratos Technologies

Steamboat Springs, Colorado

United States of America

"I am willing to tap my root down to the deepest, darkest part of myself, where I've hidden self-doubt and fear too ugly for others to see; and just with the soft but determined root tip, gently break it up so that the light gets in. Greatness, to me, is true happiness. It is the willingness to 'know thyself' completely and to persevere- not more special than, but just as extraordinarily, as a single piece of fruit ripened on a vine, in service to the world."

-Teresa 'Tree' Rogerson

Landscape Designer

Sri Lanka

"Greatness is the ability to inspire others by your actions."

-Udana Warnakulasooriya

Senior Merchandiser Hirdaramani International Exports

Dallas, Texas
United States of America

"Greatness is believing in yourself that you can achieve anything in life no matter what obstacles are put in your path. Greatness is the beat in your heart, the drive in your spirit, and the mindset to evolve into a better you."

-LaVida Harris

Executive Assistant to Publisher at KRAVE Magazine

Seed 43
PEARL OF GREAT PRICE

PEARL OF GREAT PRICE

There is one thing I know for certain. This is that knowing who created you, who started all of life, is the most important thing you will ever discover. Everything about who you are, who you were and who you are to become stems from this exceptional discovery. Several journey throughout life, wandering from here to there, searching for God or for something or someone with God-like characteristics, all the while He is within us, waiting to be utilized and to communicate. What are you willing to sacrifice, to give up, to sell, to trade in, in order to have a one on one in-person meeting with God. Is there anything you would want to keep or would you give it all up? This answer must be established within you. Your God-level of use, greatness, and spiritual power will oftentimes reflect your sacrifice. Thankfully our God is full of grace, mercy, kindness, love and generosity. He has given us access to all things, to have dominion over all the Earth. The world has been placed in our hands for the ruling and the taking. He's provided for us everything we need and more.

- **Seed Description:** The price and awareness for Greatness. The price and awareness for the attention of the Greatness Giver.

- **Soil:** Plant this awareness into your life mission as you pursue that which you believe you were placed here to do.

- **Water:** It's always smart to way the cost before you take action on anything. It's even smarter to ask God for guidance.

- **Oxygen:** We are born with the attention of God. It is during life that we must decide if we want to maintain that attention and nurture that relationship or drift off into a world that continues to seek for something yet never finds it.

- **Temperature:** Everyone is different. There are multiple levels of greatness. Everyone has the ability to be used divinely while some may be used more than others. I believe this is decided upon by God.

- **Light/Darkness:** Many names come to mind who stood out over centuries because of their greatness, Albert Einstein, Martin Luther King Jr., Nikola Tesla, Ludwig van Beethoven and several more. All of which endured some type of sacrifice, isolation, illness, scrutiny or loneliness. There is great price to pay for certain levels of greatness. You must decide what you are really to endure for your own.

- **Dormancy:** On the path of your discovering your own greatness, there will be moments of dormancy when you feel like none of it has a purpose. This feeling comes from the fact that there aren't many around you who are aware of what has been revealed to you, so it's almost like being the only one in the classroom with the right answer. This dormancy must be short-lived. Greatness doesn't have to include all. Instead it often separates, for a purpose. That purpose is to lead.

- **Germination:** Support its growth by remaining truthful to yourself and what it is you hear from within. It will never be about what you hear from the outside. Your greatest moments of power, your highest thoughts, your brightest ideas, your most intimate communication with God, will all start within you.

Omaha, Nebraska
United States of America

"Greatness is maximizing your best gifts and challenging your worst fears. Greatness is finding, seeking and vigorously doing, those things that only you can do - immediately and wherever you are at in life. Greatness trusts, hopes, believes, bears, endures, and takes action. Greatness improves and grows, mobilizing and begetting greatness. Greatness focuses on service, opportunity, value in all of its manifestations; sharing, contribution, and wonder, and does not become attached."

-Karen Moore

Entrepreneur

Sweden

"Greatness, to me, is the ability to step outside of one's ego and see the big picture, to seek solutions that serve as many as possible (in all kinds of areas), while enjoying life as much as possible."

-Nadja C. Martinsson

Writer | Translator | Consultant | Global Validator

San Diego, California

United States of America

"Greatness is an identifiable attribute which transcends beyond success, power and wealth. The recognition of greatness, while both humbling and empowering; is bestowed upon us by the individual lives we change and the world we touch. Greatness shows us how we persevere through our darkest hour and sheds light on our brightest future. Although the achievement of greatness has no time table; once accomplished, it most certainly withstands the test of time."

-Gil Yarbrough

US Navy Naval Officer

London, England
United Kingdom

"Greatness to me means accepting that every individual is unique, special and born with special talents, which when developed can help us all to maximize our potential and be the best we can."

-Confident Queen Genny

Confidence Builder | Feel Good Factor Coach

BE BOLD.

We are greater than what our minds have been taught and we have access to more than what we see.

Atlanta, Georgia
United States of America

"Greatness is the ability to influence your today; while leveraging your past to make an impact to your future"

-Seane L. Shaw

CEO at It's A Mouth Full

Guatemala City
Guatemala

"Greatness is listening to yourself and doing something about it."

-Arturo Jaar

CEO VitCast

Jamaica

"Greatness is to the very best in your life and career, yet humble. Greatness allows us to achieve the state of self mastery that gives us peace of mind. This is when you're able to travel the road of life that you choose. Greatness allows you riches but is able to care for the less fortunate. Greatness allows us to see all human beings as brother and sisters of one Universal Life Force. Greatness allows us to be always loving and kind to all."

-Aubryn E.A Smith

Senior Analyst, Data Center Technologies

Beach Park, Illinois

United States of America

"Greatness means the ability to overcome every obstacle created that detours you from the path to success. It also means to use the God-given gift within to sow into people's lives."

-Lanise Harris

Student | Entrepreneur

Seed 44
SPEAK AND THE CLOUDS
WILL OPEN

SPEAK AND THE CLOUDS WILL OPEN

You have not because you ask not. It seems as if no one acknowledges the power of speaking and the emergency of communication. Just about everything we acquire and receive in life was made possible via some form of speaking or communication. When you're being interviewed for a job in person, you respond to questions by speaking a response. When you're at a restaurant ordering food, you give the waiter your order by speaking. The act of speaking governs nations, inspires, builds, destroys and heals. It's a powerful weapon that we use loosely, and rarely in the way we should. A familiar scripture in the Bible says "Speak things that are not as though they were", which means there's power, access and authority to create what isn't already, to put in place that which is out of place, to change systems and reconstruct what isn't working. So much is being said these days by millions of people yet very little is being manifested. What are we speaking? What are we talking about that is so important but not making a difference in anyone's life.

Today you must evaluate the voice within you and what needs to come out of you when called upon to share. Someone needs to hear "You can do it, don't give up", someone needs to know there is more to life than the hard times they've experienced. You not only need to speak into their lives but also into your own. Speak to your dreams, your visions, your goals, shout out loud the things you desire. Tell that career it is yours. Speak success to your business, health to your body, peace to your soul, togetherness to your family. Speak dear friend, speak. Speak and release the supernatural sounds within you so they can work in the realm where everything is possible.

- **Seed Description:** Speak things into existence.

- **Soil:** Plant this into daily life but especially into pursuing the desires of your heart.

- **Water:** Water this by communicating with yourself constantly. Not out loud in public though, that might cause a few stares. The more often you hear something, the more it stays with you. The more you're reminded of it, the more likely you will be encouraged to go after it.

- **Oxygen:** Notice how most ideas, creations and goals are spoken of before they actually come to fruition. Speaking releases it into the atmosphere which then opens up the realm of productivity to bring it to pass. You need to release it out of your mouth first, this I know.

- **Temperature:** You will need faith and boldness to operate this seed. Those around you may not understand you and some may even question your sanity. In the past many people have verbally shared with me that I was too out there with my ideas, my goals, my writings, my business ventures, my thinking, my pursuits and my vision. Now those same people are sending me their resumes to be hired.

- **Light/Darkness:** Passion makes you share your dreams and aspirations with others, you want them to know. When you share it you activate the law of attraction, yet there's more to be done for it to become your reality. Speaking it births it, you still have to nurture and raise it with research, preparation, dedication, action and process.

- **Dormancy:** There are times of dormancy and during these times you must wait. While waiting you must prepare and always remain ready. Truly, anything can happen at any moment, so before you speak it, be ready to take make room and the proper alterations in your life needed for it to arrive.

- **Germination:** Support its growth by making a vocal declaration of the things you are pursuing and desire to see in your life. You can even start right now by speaking it out to yourself, go ahead, just release it. Look back into history upon those who spoke bold statements, speeches and future ideas that all have been produced in some way and manifested into our present reality today.

Indianapolis, Indiana
United States of America

"To me, greatness is an achievement in one's life when you have shed all worry, fear, doubt and disbelief and you can just be. You are at peace with the world, with everyone and everything in it and the world sees it. People emulate what they admire."

-David A. Rice Jr.

Worldwide Filters, LLC

Newcastle

Australia

"For me greatness is being able to positively impact the lives of as many people as possible. Creating and using wealth to the advantage of all who cross my path. Having the freedom to give freely without compromise. That will be great!"

-Andrew Fenwick

Owner Optimum Health | Wellness Coach

Albany, Georgia

United States of America

"Greatness isn't the ability to say what you have, but rather to say what you are doing with what you have."

-Haryl Dabney

Public Relations at L2Networks Corp.

Denmark

"Greatness is when your life forms a complete circle of success with your family, job and friends."

-Steen Meldgaard

Head of Sales & Marketing

BE WISE.

The more you study people, the more information and details you will have in order to influence their decisions as well as know their next move.

Indonesia

"Firstly, Greatness means we could be our selves at any occasion in any time! Secondly, Greatness means we could immediately shoot 'Should you have any querries I would be more than happy to assist!' Thirdly, Greatness could quickly be responding our relatives such as 'You look so cool with your recent clothes style! Fourthly, Greatness could express our special thanks to our parents that had been protecting us when we were still being a little child running around the grass garden! Fifthly, Greatness is feeling sexy at a glance when we have been drinking the Royal Moody Wines in front of our colleagues!"

-Bony Fasius

Export

Seoul

KOREA

"A man's life can be valuated by the legacy he remains for the world."

-Oh Chang Yeop

Founder & CEO of A

Tampa, Florida
United States of America

"Greatness is the unique moment where something or someone arrives to a pinnacle place of perfection. For just that moment, nothing is missing, nothing is broken and nothing can make it anymore quintessential. Greatness is not self-sustaining nor everlasting. Time will move forward and the scramble to reach greatness begins again."

-Ebony T. Grimsley

Owner of Above Promotions Company

Seed 45
THE GIFT BESIDE YOU

THE GIFT BESIDE YOU

Though our world often classifies individuals as powerful or feeble, beautiful or average, smart or senseless, and a variety of other comparisons, we must remember that each and every person is a unique creation. No matter who they are, what they've done or did not do, there is still an ultimate purpose for them being granted the breath of life. We are all gifts from above but we lack in this awareness, rarely allowing ourselves to meditate and research its legitimacy. Society has carefully separated us to where we often dislike one another over a single issue. This is not the mind of greatness. Our similarities far outweigh our differences. All of us, you, me, the person beside you on the phone, on the train, in line, at school, at work, on the bus, in the car, wherever, are all gifts to the Earth. Words alone won't do us any good until we investigate our spiritual and internal net worth, discovering the investment by the Creator, and the expected return on the investment. Yes, we are different, not everyone acts the same or looks the same. We differ on many things but let it be known that we originate from one family, one human race that will always come together in our darkest hour. You are a gift to the world and so is the person beside you. Recognizing all the gifts around you daily will give you access to great wisdom.

- **Seed Description:** Awareness of the value of others.

- **Soil:** Plant this into all of your human relationships.

- **Water:** Water this seed by giving attention to the thoughts, ideas, cares and lives of those around you. Opening up your life to be a part of another.

- **Oxygen:** Sometimes a simple greeting, gesture, smile or a "Hello" can make someone's day brighter. Most people really do want to feel included or at least acknowledged. Don't be afraid to leave a door open for someone or to smile when no one else seems to be.

- **Temperature:** The media has had a field day making the masses believe that we're all afraid of each other and that no one wants to be bothered by the other. This is such a lie, don't believe it. I've had the privilege of bringing people together all over the world from all walks of life and to this day, I know for a fact that people really do want to connect with others, to learn, to grow and to find commonalities.

- **Light/Darkness:** Some people have no one around that takes time to listen to them or show interest in their lives, causing loneliness and a lack of hope. Show people that they matter and they will spread that fire across the globe, one person at a time.

- **Dormancy:** This seed should not go dormant. Even when we argue and have disagreements, it is imperative that we remember the value of others. Our world has consumed us with so many gadgets and entertainment to where we have almost forgotten about the most important things in life, those things that originate from within that cannot be purchased.

- **Germination:** Support its growth by investing more time in the lives of other people. It can be as simple as asking someone about their day or giving someone a compliment on their clothes or as minor as pushing the floor button for someone on an elevator, I love doing that. Remind humanity that there are still people on this planet who actually care. This is more important than you know and a must for true greatness. Showing this firsthand cancels out all the nonsense we see and hear broadcasted daily.

Los Angeles, California

United States of America

"Greatness is the ability to take advantage of opportunities presented as a result of my preparation for a time such as this. Purposely developing diverse skills, building strategic relationships and gaining confidence positions is greatness."

-Eleanor Beasley

Founder and CEO Eleanor Beasley CTP, Business Banking
Consultants

London, England
United Kingdom

"Planting good seeds requires our perception to do its best towards our request. Just as we were perfectly formed within the womb (disabilities and all) shows our desire to push forward through the good and bad times. Choosing to flourish is a step we can all make or take. We can only be as great and mighty to ourselves first, in order to spread this everlasting joy and need to share through the gifts we have. This sharing is what connects us plus gives us a spark to work or link with each other to continue to grow and nurture our inspirations. As each one feeds the other mentally or physically, desires and longings become formed into reality. Let us therefore place our best foot forward and feel the greatness that you are...you'll be so glad you did! More love, more peace & kindness is a wealth of greatness worth creating."

-Hellen Adom

CEO Elle Productions

Chicago, Illinois
United States of America

"Greatness is being. It is serving others to the best of one's ability through love and compassion."

-Eric Somogyi

Student at Columbia College Chicago

Stockholm

Sweden

"Greatness is having a natural ability to add value, to contribute, to share happiness, to make others feel better and to have a positive influence in any environment. It is living the life with greater manners!"

-Max Mohammadhassan Mohammadi

CEO and Founder Sky of ARTS

BE GREAT.

There is no template to being great, the greatest of us all didn't do it by being liked by everyone else, they did it by being themselves and then taking their unique brand of "them" to great extents.

Colorado Springs, Colorado

United States of America

"Greatness means to live full-out and full on your purpose for life. Everyone has the seed of Greatness within them and once the barriers of fear are overcome, great things will happen."

-Dan Weigold

Associate Coach at Business Success Coach Network

Zambia

"Greatness means achieving extra-ordinary and unique feats that are useful and purposeful, which works to resolve, uplift, change, develop, uplift or motivate an individual, group or institution."

-Emmanuel Chilekwa

Business Owner | Development Consultant

New York, New York
United States of America

"Greatness is just simply being who you are and honoring yourself by living in your personal truth. Yes there are many truths and paths to greatness, but which one you choose will be the one to bring you joy. There are many people to meet on the path of greatness; family, friends, and those to become friends. Greatness is inclusive and honors those along the path, even if the light on the path is dim, yet to be illuminated by the sun."

-Hillis Pugh

Entrepreneur | Author of "Thank You Thursday"

Campinas, Sao Paulo

Brazil

"To be willing to help another without the intention of charging back favors later on."

-Tiago Tex Pine

Game Producer | Designer

Seed 46
NOT BY YOURSELF

NOT BY YOURSELF

Life is a composite of many things, a coming together of ideas, people, places, circumstances, events and happenings. We were never meant to experience life alone. We are given parents at birth, then family, friends, schoolmates, co-workers, spouses and more. In addition to our natural cohabitants, we have a spiritual family as well, a host of angels always alert to protect us, and a God who orchestrates even the worse situations in life to turn out for our good. You may think you're alone at this moment, but truly my friend, you're not. We must understand our connection to all people, to all creation. We must enter into the realm of solitude in order to reconnect with the simple, the obvious, and the spiritual, where impossibilities don't exist.

Too many distractions keep us from ourselves. Go to the deeper place within you, this is not only your escape to find peace, it is also your power to discover the truth. We all originate from the same, therefore we are all united in this no matter how separate or how distant we appear. You're not by yourself. Open your heart, open your mind, open your world to the good things we share as brothers and sisters. Your spirit will attract the amazing when you do. Not only will your entire world change, you'll have the power and understanding within you to change the world yourself.

- **Seed Description:** Embrace your human and spiritual family.

- **Soil:** Plant this into days when you feel alone. The more you open yourself to appreciate those around you and those watching over you, the more the universe will open itself up to whatever you desire.

- **Water:** Water this seed by seeking a closer relationship with God and the things of God. The closer you are to God, the closer you are to people.

- **Oxygen:** Use this seed to free yourself from the preconceived, nonproductive ideas and misconstrued perceptions that others and the media have perpetuated for decades.

- **Temperature:** Observe people, places, things, and responses. I've learned that observation opens up a new world to the one that desires it. We miss so much each day, everything passes as a sound bite and then we're on to the next thing. You'll have to stop, wait, and think, more often than most, to fully take advantage of this seed.

- **Light/Darkness:** This seed is full of revelation, secrets and joy. It can also cause others to speak negatively against you, even write you off as being "out there in space". Regardless of what people think, embrace your truth and the new wisdom that gives you the advantage.

- **Dormancy:** You should always seek to discover the natural and the true supernatural as much as possible throughout life, for it is the gateway to endless wisdom. Maintaining a silent awareness of this is the key, never dormant, but simmering quietly.

- **Germination:** Support its growth through meditation, worship, research, observation, as well as by Listening With Golden Ears (reference: Seed 11).

Jacksonville, Florida

United States of America

"Greatness is resiliency, it overcomes trials, and tribulations. In order to achieve greatness one must remain individualistic."

-Gerald Joseph

Blogger | Stylist | Social Entrepreneur

Oslo

Norway

"Greatness is all good visions converted into action! So, everyone is good enough. In a complex world with ever increasing focus on perfection we must never forget that every one is his own genius. Open your mind, think alternatively and you will see all individuals have an inherent power to make a difference."

-Flemming Wagner

Executive Chairman at ASV Solar AS

New York, New York
United States of America

"Greatness...is about having the courage to lead others away from their baser selves of hate, greed, etc. and towards the truth of our purpose: to collaborate, love deeply and enjoy life together in peace. You set the example because you have fought that battle within yourself and won. You have had the courage to stare at the end of your life, and prepare a legacy starting now. You chose to fight for the good in this world and in people. Greatness in summary... is a choice, it is positive and lifts up those around you as you proceed on your life's journey."

-Emily Correa

Life/Business Coach | Founder Vida Linda Coaching

Croatia

"Humbleness is the main seed of greatness."

-Katarina Jagic

President Croatian Small Business Union

BE BOLD.

Observe and learn more than what is expected or scheduled.

Atlanta, Georgia

United States of America

"Greatness is having the determination to never allow failure to be an option. Greatness is more than the accolades that the world system sets up. Greatness is knowing early on that God has set you up for greatness and the average status quo just won't do. Knowing where your greatness derives from makes you great."

-Shari L. Capers

"Beautiful Homes Now" Real Estate Broker

Entrepreneur

Richmond Hill, Ontario

Canada

"Greatness is the ability to accept who you are, to be aware that "the sky is the limit" and that you can achieve whatever goal you set as long as you are willing to stay the course, to have the tenacity to hold on and never let go. Greatness is overcoming the challenges, the negativities and the disappointments that we face daily in striving to be the very best we can be, but more importantly, extending a helping hand to others along the way."

-Eulalie Walling-Sampson

President at Loring Enterprise

Menomonee Falls, Wisconsin
United States of America

"Greatness to me means that I recognize without a shadow of a doubt that "I can do all things through Christ who strengthens me", Philippians 4:13. And, to remember that greatness has nothing to do with one particular individual but the impartation of significance displayed in the lives of many."

-Shontina Gladney

Entrepreneur | Life Transition Expert

Qatar

"Greatness is forgiving, greatness is equality, no rich no poor, treating everyone equal, treating everyone as human. Greatness is spreading love without any discrimination. Being calm and content, being humble, being helpful. Following & showing others the proper path of truth & love and also to realize your purpose of being on earth

-Parminder Jasdhol

Director | Producer

Seed 47

ACTIVATE YOUR HEIRS

ACTIVATE YOUR HEIRS

I believe the true sign of success is when you can use your own life and success to make someone else a success. We have the power and influence to push others into greatness just by supporting what they do and what they believe. Assisting someone in achieving their goals, helping them turn an idea into reality, or even just encouraging them is a part of the process of activating your heirs. This simply means using your life, your presence, your existence, to benefit those coming after you. Motivation alone can change someone's life. Lending a hand at the right time can inspire another to change the world. We must take heed to this process and be aware of its importance. Establishing a life, a foundation, of inspiration, motivation and charity to others, is how you build and grow a priceless estate of abundance. This produces heirs of every race, every gender and background, which duplicates itself over and over, heir to heir, generation to generation.

- **Seed Description:** Use your life to produce inspiration in others.

- **Soil:** Plant this is into your daily life, career pursuits and life purpose.

- **Water:** Water this seed by accepting that your life was not meant just for you. The things you do and say have impact and influence on other people, therefore you have the power to build or destroy.

- **Oxygen:** People follow those that inspire them, motivate them or those that carry a message or mission that resonates within them. It is important that we know what message our life is delivering to others on a daily basis.

- **Temperature:** We live in a society that seems to be slowly disconnecting from the value of human life. You must be a game changer in this area. We can't let the negative outshine the positive. Greatness must leap forth out of you and you must be bold enough to share it every chance you get.

- **Light/Darkness:** Most people are looking for guidance. This is obvious through magazine subscriptions, book sales, conference & seminar attendance, and so forth. This serves as evidence that there are heirs waiting to be activated to further spread your message throughout the Earth. Do not take this for granted. This is your moment to lead by example.

- **Dormancy:** You should always remain aware of the power of your life. Dormancy is never an issue once introduced to this awareness.

- **Germination:** Support its growth through observation and by being all that you believe you were born to be. Seek out everything that can make you greater. Live as if any day could be the last.

Las Vegas, Nevada

United States of America

"Greatness is unapologetically, knowing your identity in Christ. Greatness, is accepting responsibility for your past and your own problems. Greatness is making a decision when God is waiting for you to make the right choice, moving forward, erasing fear, doubt and frustration. Greatness is moving into a dimension staying the course with a no quit attitude and fulfilling any dream that enters my mind, body and soul."

-Nichole Henderson

Owner of Victorious Beginnings Behavioral Center

Cyprus

"Greatness is in every one of us. What separates those who have tapped into greatness from those who have not is passion. Passion fuels us, drives us, motivates us, empowers us. Opportunities present themselves consistently when passion is present. Once our passion is pursued, greatness naturally follows for one is not without the other."

-Christina Makrides

Founder of Cyprus Loyalty Clubs

Nigeria

"Greatness is a progressive ability that ignites ones strength to push more for the top at all time and never stop to change from one positive level point to another."

-Taiwo Adeleke

Video/Photo Journalist

BE WISE.

Greatness starts from within but is an example that is witnessed by others.

Waikato

New Zealand

"Greatness is choosing clear values that you truly believe in, and acting on those values consistently. In business I believe those Values of Greatness involve serving people in such a way that not only are they better off, but the world is a better place for you having been here. Acting on Values of Greatness will often mean challenging current processes, beliefs and misconceptions, regardless of the personal price of doing so. And remember Greatness does not equate to popularity."

-Chris Hanlon

Business Author

San Francisco, California

United States of America

"Greatness is the infinite effort of bringing out your best!
Everyone possesses the potential for greatness!"

-Beverly Black Johnson

CEO Gumbo for the Soul International

Rotterdam
Netherlands

"Being great implies knowing to differentiate good from bad. If you do the right things right, respecting your environment and learn from it, Greatness is a logical result."

-Stefan van Eerde

Entrepreneur | Founder of Direct Students

Cincinnati, Ohio

United States of America

"Greatness is the ability to inspire others selflessly, helping them to see that they can achieve and accomplish whatever they put their minds to."

-Teri Cheatham

Founder of Combined Networking LLC

Seed 48
GATHER THE WOOD

GATHER THE WOOD

You were born to bring light to the dark places of life and the dark places of the world. In the midst of living our daily lives, we have to remain aware that we are agents of change. We are responsible for finding out what the needs are and how we can help make a difference. It should also be our desire to tell others about these needs while recruiting more people to join in on the efforts. This is to Gather The Wood. The more wood we gather, the greater the flame will be and the more the fire of doing good can spread. Gather the wood when you see injustice, when you know something isn't fair and others are suffering because of it. Gather the wood when people lack knowledge that you have, so you can share it to expand their lives. Teach your children and your family to gather the wood to light up the world with hope, charity and inspiration, we can't afford to ever let the flame burn out. As long as God allows the trees to grow, we must continue to gather the wood.

- **Seed Description:** Spread hope, knowledge, and philanthropy.

- **Soil:** Plant this into every moment made available to you to make a difference in a situation or someone's life.

- **Water:** Water this seed by understanding that we live in a world where hope appears to be withering away and where change is now mandatory.

- **Oxygen:** You are an agent of change or you desire to become one. This book reached your hands because you attracted it to your life. You have been chosen to gather the wood.

- **Temperature:** This seed requires much solitude and prayer, for it is the atmosphere within you that strengthens it. There will be plenty of voices on the outside but you must only listen to those with wisdom, knowledge and understanding.

- **Light/Darkness:** This seed will elevate your life to a point where you may feel as if you are on top of a mountain. It is at that moment when you can look down and see just how sad, frustrated, stressed, depressed and lonely several people are around the world. Use this information strategically to make things better for someone else.

- **Dormancy:** This seed should never experience dormancy. Even when you don't feel like using it, that is the precise time when you should.

- **Germination:** Support its growth by surrounding yourself with others who gather the wood. You will remain encouraged and empowered by those who share the same spirit and mission.

Snellville, Georgia

United States of America

"I believe that true greatness lies in achieving excellence while embracing humility... putting others ahead of self."

-Robert Davis

Owner at Davis Advertising, Inc.

Riga
Latvia

"Greatness is to be free, with good reputation, and to help others to reach the same."

-Valdis Tilgalis

Researcher

Memphis, Tennessee
United States of America

"Reaching out with love and concern to those in need, no matter what their situation, or yours, exemplifies greatness. Your help, even in a small way, gives them strength and courage to face their situation and move forward. One can make excuses, or they can reach out. The great ones will do whatever it takes to reach out.."

-Jana Cardona

Executive Director BNI

Toronto, Ontario
Canada

"Greatness is actively, consciously and passionately living the life you want."

-Jonathan Lau

Senior Legal Counsel at TVO

BE GREAT.

Your greatness will always be tested through pain or power.

New York, New York

United States of America

"Greatness is the ability to understand someone's dream and be able to influence, inspire and make the dreamers see how bright he/she will shine for humanity. While enduring along the way their pain and sacrifices until their moment comes, then humbly moving aside to admire and applaud their extraordinary greatness."

-Oscar Pinella

CEO/President Dalios Music Publishing, Inc & Winners Music Group, Inc

Trinidad and Tobago

"Greatness is the ability to be true to you, despite what happens, to be your divine self, manifest your vision and expand your beauty into the lives of those around you."

-Ursaline McLeod

Fashion Designer

Hazel Crest, Illinois
United States of America

"Greatness to me is realizing your God-given gift and giving God all the glory for what ever that gift may be. Greatness is helping and sharing with others so all whom follow their hopes and dreams can experience what it feels like to be accomplished in their journey."

-Oscar Warren Jr.

Owner of D'Luvv Records & Entertainment

Seed 49
PRODUCE. PRODUCE. PRODUCE.

PRODUCE. PRODUCE. PRODUCE.

No one will ever truly know you were here unless you leave something behind. Whether it be a creation of some sort or the way your life inspired another, you must produce. It is our natural instinct, our shared gift, our common denominator to manifest ideas and thoughts into reality. We must continue to produce every year, something that will outlast our lifetime. Whether its how we raise our families, writing a book, motivating the youth, or encouraging a co-worker. What are you producing? Be careful not to spend your entire life watching the show. We all have a part to play in this production. It doesn't matter how large or small the role, it's still yours, and it's mandatory that you deliver.

- **Seed Description:** Produce your legacy.

- **Soil:** Plant this into your present and future, giving thought to what it is your life is producing and evaluating the impact.

- **Water:** Pay attention to your ideas and your biggest thoughts. These give access to a realm of productivity and genius that many stray away from due to fear and lack of knowledge. You must invest time in the higher you for this seed to survive.

- **Oxygen:** Study the lives of those you consider legendary, those you admire, and pay close attention to their journey if you can obtain such information through research. Every day is an open door to walk into the extraordinary. It's all a matter of perception, ideas, focus and strategy. The more aware you are of your inner genius, which is God, the more you will produce.

- **Temperature:** Though I believe we are all born with several destinations already set before us, we still have the power to expand this by pursuing the impossible. Boldness and faith can lead you into realms where angels are dispatched to do the supernatural on your behalf at any moment. Accompanied by immovable focus, you will inevitably become an unstoppable force in your lifetime, being used as a major conduit to the dreams and an unlimited creator. Steve jobs comes to mind, he perfected this seed in his business life and we continue to enjoy the fruits of it.

- **Light/Darkness:** Those who are aware of the power of this seed live a different life. It becomes hard to keep so much light inside. It eventually breaks through own its own, manifesting externally in various ways. We were created as creators. When we don't create, we lose parts of our soul and we slowly alienate this divine characteristic.

- **Dormancy:** Once of age, maturity and awareness, this seed should be productive in your life daily. In the midst of day to day living, we are unaware of our time frame left.

Knowing this, you should always be preparing for the next opportunity to expand or reinvent your legacy.

- **Germination:** Support its growth by tuning in to your purpose, the reason you believe you were put here on Earth, at this moment and time. Your awareness keeps you alert, reminding the universe that you remain ready to take care of business.

Chicago, Illinois
United States of America

"Greatness to me is reaching one's fullest self-potential and ability that one could possibly acquire to complete a goal. It's the immeasurable limit of an individual's will and determination to conquer a task or defeat an immense challenge, in hopes to receive appreciation for the goals achieved, that he or she was told it was impossible to do. It's everything stored inside of us that we bring out that allows us to shine like no other."

-Aaron Robinson

President/Editor of Consciousness Magazine

San Jose

Costa Rica

"Greatness is the ability to take the good part of every situation. To care, love, learn, laugh and have a great day. To transmit this energy to all around you, making a positive impact in their lives."

-Johnny Tarcica

Founder and CEO at Empleos

2:00pm - Time to be Great.

Arkadelphia, Arkansas
United States of America

"Greatness is something we all possess. It is shown in many ways. Nobody should ever feel like they have a smaller amount of it than any other person. Each and every one of us is beautiful and unique no matter what."

-Danielle Savage

Artist | Author | Humanitarian

Toronto, Ontario
Canada

"Greatness is to be here now with all of your being, forever present in the moment."

-Laurie Grant

Managing Consultant

BE BOLD.

Be open-mined enough to seek out the similarities that unite us and be brave enough to share them with the entire world.

Albany, Georgia
United States of America

"Greatness is knowing that you have climbed the highest mountain and overcome the biggest obstacle while never giving up. It is also striving for the best but not settling for less."

-Parshandatha Zerest Davis Jr.

LEAP Sustainment Manager

Italy

"Greatness can be identified with two very simple words: love and forgiveness."

-Valeria D'Ellena

EF Leader presso EF Education First

from New York, New York
United States of America

*"Greatness is knowing that you are a very powerful person--
regardless of your financial status or ethnicity. You can
achieve all of your goals and realize your power to give back
to others in your community, especially   young people."*

-Dachell McSween

Founder, A Fountain of Youth, Inc.

from Brussels

Belgium

"Greatness is to create, help, cross your borders and help other cross theirs. All this with humility and sense of humour."

-Bernard de Burlin

General Manager IPM IMMO

Seed 50
PATIENCE

PATIENCE

Greatness is a journey, it's an experience, it's an idea, it's a lifestyle and it's a decision. You can't obtain it overnight, you can't buy it, it'll never go on sale and it's never free. In life there is a time for everything. The wise learn that while preparing and pursuing, you must also master patience. Patience is the hardest thing to keep and easiest thing to lose. You'll never be a success without it and greatness won't hang around if you don't learn how to manage it. It's tough to wait, especially when your eyes are glued to the lives and progression of others.

Look above dear friend, toward the sky, not eye level to where you see someone else, but to the clouds, on top of the mountain, where you belong and where you'll always receive instruction, looking down to see the people, observing the world, so you know exactly where and when to plant, water, grow and share the seeds of greatness.

- **Seed Description:** Patience

- **Soil:** Plant this into times of anxiety or frustration, when you want things rushed and faster than they should be.

- **Water:** This seed must be practiced. You'll need to put yourself in positions where you have to be patient, that's the only way to water it.

- **Oxygen:** Some people have no patience, this is not good. Several appear erratic the majority of the time. It's best that you do not associate with this type but instead the opposite, someone who embodies a patient spirit that you can learn from. To master patience is to find peace with timing.

- **Temperature:** Patience is learned. It's not a gift but a virtue, one that can be enhanced throughout life. It comes with knowledge, maturity and peace of mind. Once you obtain it, share it, because many will experience great loss and disappointment without it.

- **Light/Darkness:** As far as your pursuits, be wise to know when patience is needed and when action must take place immediately. Several suffer and miss clear opportunities by confusing the two. The key is preparation and a keen sense of timing. When an opportunity arises, patience should only be used if you truly believe you need to prepare more before making the next move.

- **Dormancy:** We should aim to teach our kids patience at an early age. Though it seems we live in a microwave society, the reality is, for most parts of life, we don't. This seed will not experience dormancy. It is used daily, in multiple ways, even when we aren't aware of it. When ripe, gather lots of patience to last throughout each season. You will not be able to survive without it.

- **Germination:** Support its growth by observing that which causes you to become impatient. Create situations where you would normally lose your patience so you can practice growing your patience. To truly become great, you must proactively challenge yourself, even more so than the natural obstacles that will come against you in life.

Houston, Texas

United States of America

"The Greatest Loss; is leaving this earth, and not using our "Seeds" for their pre-set course in the Earth. To me this is the greatest thing we can learn from, this book by Germaine Moody."

-Dennis Ford Jr.

CEO Devine Global Solutions

BE Become Endless

Enjoy more books by Germaine Moody.

Discover Wisdom
100 Days of Inspiration and Power

In "Discover Wisdom" Germaine shares one hundred days of time-sensitive wisdom to inspire, inform and equip everyone who desires to live higher, dream bigger and accomplish more on their journey of life. Through experience and observation, awareness and adaptation, trials and triumphs, this inspirational and transitional day to day self-motivating masterpiece will prove to be an asset in the lives of individuals for generations to come. ©2013

The Quotes
2nd Edition

Germaine Moody shares over 600 of his original quotes in this remarkable and personal compilation that continues to inspire, equip, inform and motivate millions around the world. ©2013

...books continued.

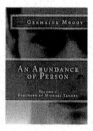

An Abundance of Person vol. 1
You were created from genius and born to greatness.

Volume 1 of "An Abundance Of Person" is a three year writing
journey along a remarkably enlightening yet lonely and draining
path Germaine Moody had to take. From the depths of his soul,
this writing exhaled then stretched him beyond himself, leaving
him empty while completely filled. This book aggressively though
passionately unearths the beauty, power and genius within us all to
become everything that we are created to be. X-raying the
physical, mental, emotional and spiritual....as he relates to these as
the four layers of a person. It's an introduction to self. A realization
and awareness of You, yet with no ending... ©2011

CPSIA information can be obtained
at www.ICGtesting.com
Printed in the USA
LVOW03s1541251017
553730LV00012BA/1006/P